GARDENS *of the* GARDEN STATE

GARDENS *of the* GARDEN STATE

Nancy Berner and Susan Lowry

Photographs by Gemma and Andrew Ingalls

THE MONACELLI PRESS

Published in the United States by The Monacelli Press.

Library of Congress Control Number: 2014936807

ISBN 9781580933742

Designed by Susan Evans, Design per se

Printed in China

The Monacelli Press

236 West 27th Street

New York, New York 10001

www.monacellipress.com

ACKNOWLEDGMENTS

First and foremost, thank you to all the garden owners, for their great generosity and kindness in welcoming us in to their gardens, often more than once.

There are so many people to whom we owe gratitude and thanks; what follows is only a partial list: Diane Botnick, Austin Buck, Sally Emery, Richard Hartlage, Barbara Israel, Mary Jasch, Pam Jeanes, Marta McDowell, Shelby Doggett Mellick, Bill Noble, Laura Palmer, Leslie Parness, Mrs. Lois Poinier, Alison Potter, Nancy Pyne, Leigh Sorensen, Quill Teal-Sullivan, Judith Tankard, and Lisa Weilbacker.

We are grateful for the time that the professional gardeners took with us, especially Mike Tober, Clive Deeble, Heder Lopez ,and Joe Thomas, as well as that stellar duo Michael and Hilary Clayton.

We very much appreciate the help we received from the stewards of New Jersey's great public gardens, including: Jim Avens, Suzanne Broullon, Deborah Bryant, George Butrus, Letitia Clark, Bruce Crawford, Nancy Fadynich, Charles Fischer, Rich Flynn, Matt Gundy, Brendan Huggins, Liz Johnson, Frank Juliano, Allen and Hella Lacy, Joan Scott Miller, John Morse, Steve Murray, Joan Ryder, Linda Sercus, Pamela Wilson.

We especially thank our patient and encouraging editor, Elizabeth White at The Monacelli Press; our designer, Susan Evans of Design per se; and, finally, our photographers, Gemma and Andrew Ingalls.

CONTENTS

INTRODUCTION

A number of years ago we were invited to give a talk to the members of a garden club in Somerset County. New Jersey was then terra incognita. Once we were off the highway, we found ourselves on quiet country roads, driving through well-kept woods interspersed with rolling fields; every now and then, sets of stone pillars in varying states of repair would indicate a driveway. We were in hunt country, though we did not know it at the time. After the talk, we asked the club members if there were any gardens in the area to visit and we were directed to the Leonard J. Buck Garden, where we spent a blissful hour among the choice specimens. It dawned on us that we were in a place that must rank in the forefront of the nation's rock and woodland gardens, and that it was set in countryside that epitomized a rural ideal. That was the beginning of our fascination with New Jersey and our first inkling that the Garden State had a deep store of garden treasures.

For those of us who look to gardens as a way to explore the culture and history of a region, New Jersey is an interesting conundrum. It is the fifth smallest state in the nation and the most densely populated, yet it has been a pioneer in open space preservation and has large swaths of virtually uninhabited, preserved land, including several unique landscapes like the Great Swamp and the Pine Barrens. Its gardens are extremely varied, a reflection not so much of the wide diversity of its population, but of the quite dramatic physical differences in landscape within its modest 70 by 170 miles. In New Jersey, geography matters.

For such a small state, the topography is complex, partially because the geologic history is even more so. New Jersey was the endpoint of the last Ice Age, and glaciers swept the northern third of the state at least three times, creating unique and identifiable topographical details. Four distinct geographical regions divide the state in bands from the north to the southwest. The Appalachian Ridge and Valley, which includes the Delaware Water Gap, runs parallel to the state line along the northwestern corner and has the highest elevation at the appropriately named High Point (elevation 1,803 feet) in the Kittatinny Mountains. Running parallel just east of the Ridge and Valley is the Highlands, whose rugged terrain includes many lakes and reservoirs, tucked in among the hills, which supply water to the rest of the state. Moving east, the Highlands transition into the Piedmont region, which reaches from the New York border to Pennsylvania and then gives way to the Coastal Plain, which extends over sixty percent of New Jersey's territory. Here, the landscape includes the rich farmlands of the inner coastal plain as well as the mysterious and ecologically unique Pine Barrens and the beloved Jersey Shore.

The climate varies hugely. The average winter temperature is ten degrees colder in northern Sussex County than in Cape May County in the far south, meaning that the northwest corner of the state is hardiness zone 5b and the southeast is 7b. Ice and snow can be a big factor for gardeners in northern Sussex County, and hurricanes can be devastating for the entire state, but especially to the vulnerable shore areas, as Hurricane Sandy proved in 2012.

As befits a state that was one of the original thirteen, New Jersey has a lively and lengthy history of making gardens. We know that, before the Revolution, John Stockton of Princeton was creating a garden based on the ideas of the English poet Alexander Pope at Morven (now a historic house and garden open to the public). By the mid-nineteenth century, while the state was undergoing the same industrial expansion as the rest of the country, transitioning from an agriculture-based economy to a manufacturing-based one, its towns and villages were becoming a magnet for city dwellers looking for respite from the increasingly crowded and chaotic urban centers. In the northern part of New Jersey, New Yorkers of means moved to the state, chasing an already vanishing rural life. The expansion of the railroads aided both the industrialization of the economy and the increasing suburbanization of large parts of the state; by 1870 most of the population in New Jersey lived within ten miles of a railroad. After 1910, rail service under the Hudson River made it even easier to live in a comfortable suburb and work in the city. The opening of the Holland Tunnel in 1927, the George Washington Bridge in 1931, and the Lincoln Tunnel in 1937 only accelerated this trend.

The well-to-do towns and suburbs were often at the forefront of national land preservation movements. The nation's first planned community, Llewellyn Park, established in East Orange in 1857, attracted such celebrities as Thomas Edison, for many years the state's most famous citizen. Essex County, working with the Olmsted Brothers, established the first county park, the 360-acre Branch Brook Park, which today is distinguished by having the largest cherry tree display in the country, a magical sight in early May.

Begonias tucked into a mossy urn in a quiet border at Greenwood Gardens.

During the late nineteenth century, towns like Morristown, within comfortable commuting distance of the city, attracted a new class of plutocrats who built substantial houses on large estates. At one point Morristown was reputed to have more millionaires per square foot than New York City. As Morristown became more congested, the locus of these estates moved out into the countryside, a good number of them to the Somerset Hills. A few, like Blairsden in Peapack, a thirty-eight-room mansion matched by elaborate gardens designed by James Greenleaf, have struggled to retain their former glory, but a surprising number of estates have been carefully preserved or converted to other uses. The most ambitious of these is the 2,740-acre Duke Farms, the tobacco heiress Doris Duke's famed domain, also once adorned with gardens by Greenleaf and now turned into a state-of-the-art environmental center with miles of hiking and biking trails and a popular community garden. Duke Farms, along with twenty-one other properties, form the backbone of New Jersey's remarkable collection of historic gardens. The Garden State Gardens consortium includes twenty-two major public gardens, most of which were originally created by wealthy landowners in the early part of the twentieth century. Six of these gardens are included here, but there are many other impressive ones, such as the former Whippany Farm, now the Frelinghuysen Arboretum, which is the headquarters of Morris County's extensive park system and a hub of horticultural information and education, or the Sister Mary Grace Arboretum at Georgian Court University in Lakehurst, once the estate of George Jay Gould, son of infamous financier Jay Gould. Not surprisingly, many of these estates were designed by the major practitioners of the day. In addition to the previously mentioned James Greenleaf, Samuel Parsons Jr. and Calvert Vaux both had a hand in designing the Reeves-Reed estate, the legendary firm of Vitale and Geiffert followed Samuel Parsons Jr. at Skylands, and their successor firm Innocenti and Webel had many residential projects in New Jersey, including Dunwalke East. This tradition persists in the work of the outstanding Spanish architect Fernando Caruncho at Bird Haven Farm and of the eminent English garden designer and writer Penelope Hobhouse at Ellistan.

A particularly interesting community of gardeners existed in the Somerset Hills at the turn of the twentieth century. This period, when garden-making flourished, began just before World War I, the same era that saw the founding of the Garden Club of America. Martha Brookes Hutcheson, a pioneering landscape designer, retired from active practice in 1912 and moved to Merchiston Farm in Gladstone, where she built her own garden and wrote and proselytized about the importance of gardens in civic life. Merchiston Farm is now a public garden and hosts the Bamboo Brook Education Center of the Morris County Park System. Hutcheson's immediate neighbor and great friend was Hal Tubbs of Willowwood. Tubbs, along with his brother Robert, was building an

extensive arboretum, whose frequent visitors included Leonard Buck of Allwood (now the Leonard J. Buck Garden). Julia Newbold Cross of the Cross Estate exchanged plants with the Tubbs brothers as well. All of these gardeners shared a passion for plants; in addition to exchanging specimens among themselves, they were in touch with plant finders and specialists around the world.

This plant obsession was shared by great gardeners throughout the state. At Skylands in Sussex County, Clarence McKenzie Lewis put together an extensive series of plant collections, including rock gardens, lilacs and rare rhododendrons and azaleas. Here, Ben Blackburn got his start in a summer job before going on to do graduate work at Rutgers University, where he organized the famous shrub collection, then becoming a distinguished professor of horticulture at Drew University and, most importantly, working with the Tubbs brothers in creating the arboretum at Willowwood. Starting in the 1930s Dorothy Knippenburg was hybridizing her favorite rhododendrons at Laurelwood, while in Montclair, Howard Van Vleck gave up his career as an architect to focus on hybridizing rhododendron and azalea. The town of Montclair established the Presby Memorial Iris Gardens in 1927, which was and remains one of the premier iris gardens in the country. In the 1920s, Elizabeth C. White of Whitesbog in the New Jersey Pine Barrens, while working in her father's extensive cranberry bog business, developed with Dr. Fred Coville the commercial high-bush blueberry. New Jersey is now the country's second largest grower of blueberries.

People garden for different reasons. There are those for whom plants are the means to create beautiful spaces and environments and those for whom plants are the point.

Left: A path winding through a field of scilla 'Spring Beauty' at The Hay, Honey Farm.

Right: Espalier on the side of Lenore and Bob Rice's Tudor cottage in Short Hills.

This latter group seems to have been historically well represented in New Jersey, and the same is true today. Taking advantage of the often excellent soil and growing conditions, superb specialty nurseries dot the state, including RareFind Nursery, Well-Sweep Herb Farm, Atlock Farm, and Peony's Envy, all of which have gardens open to the public. The slogan "New Jersey Grown" appears on plant material all over the tri-state area, and Springfest, the New Jersey garden show in Sussex County, is a highlight of the early spring season.

An active tradition of garden writing began with, among others, Martha Brookes Hutcheson and also Helena Rutherford Ely (*A Woman's Hardy Garden* was a bestseller when it came out in 1903 and is still in print). Allen Lacy and Ken Druse, two of the best garden writers of their respective generations, continue this tradition: they both garden in the state, one in the north, the other in the south, and both are extraordinarily knowledgeable and passionate about plants.

Many of the garden owners featured in this book share this plant addiction. The gardeners at Hay, Honey Farm in Far Hills are a good example, as is James Golden in Kingwood Township. The varied grasses that Golden features in his garden can also be found at Fairfields, where they are the predominant design element. At Jardin de Buis, architect Andrea Filippone showcases boxwood in plantings of all sizes and shapes. At Linden Hill and at the Hereford Inlet Lighthouse, annuals have star billing, while at Kennelston Cottage and at Poodle Point, roses are shown off to perfection. And at Frog Pond, delicate spring ephemerals are displayed to great effect in the woodlands. In the garden of Clay and Pat Sutton, the plants are specially chosen with an eye on the birds and butterflies that will be passing through. On the surface, the four gardens by Richard

Hartlage might seem design-driven, yet they are clearly informed by his extensive knowledge of and deep sensitivity to plants—after all, Hartlage developed Calycanthus 'Hartlage Wine,' which we found in gardens all over the state. And at Greenwood, the state's newest public historic garden, Louis Bauer, its first director of horticulture, has created a horticultural showcase.

The twenty-nine gardens presented here are only a sampling of the rich and complex garden world of New Jersey. With such a vast array of options, the selection was necessarily personal. We chose the gardens with some attempt at geographic distribution, and we have presented them starting in the north and moving south, because geography has such an effect on how these gardens look and how they came into being. For example, the private garden in the northern part of the state has very few of the acid-loving rhododendron and azalea that we see so often in other New Jersey gardens because it is located in an area of limestone, which is an anathema to acid-loving plants. Dorothy Knippenberg turned to azalea and rhododendron because her Wayne County hillside was ideal for growing them. Buck Garden came into being because its owner was fascinated by the geology of Moggy Hollow. In addition to geography, the other essential point for us in choosing a garden is that it speaks in a voice that expresses a particular point of view, and says something to us about the people or the ideas behind the garden.

One of the great joys of preparing this book has been the number of magnificent plant specimens we have "met." We have had literally hundreds of encounters with remarkable trees and shrubs. A visit to the legendary Rutgers Gardens introduced us to some memorable witch hazels and a stunningly beautiful Kobus magnolia. The giant pecan tree at Willowwood, not to mention the historic metasequoia, created long-term memories, as did the wisteria at the Van Vleck mansion, where we also admired one of the original Edith Bogue magnolias. The smooth gray trunks of the red maples that form a remarkable allée at Grounds for Sculpture in Hamilton Township confirmed for us that trees can rival any sculpture. The February-blooming witch hazels at Hella and Allen Lacy's garden were as spectacular as any summer planting. The seven Newton Sentry maples and the magnificent 'Wolf Eyes' dogwood that we met at Ken Druse and Louis Bauer's garden were encounters that changed the way we think of both species.

Whether exploring the many outstanding gardens, meeting knowledgeable and generous gardeners or discovering new plants to admire, preparing *Gardens of the Garden State* has been an absorbing experience. And in all the varied gardens we visited we have found the calm and peace that Martha Brookes Hutcheson evoked in her book *The Spirit of the Garden*: "So let us all have gardens . . . Above all, let us have a sense of seclusion in our flowered space, that the calm and peace shall in no way be broken."

NEW JERSEY STATE BOTANICAL GARDEN AT SKYLANDS

RINGWOOD

Skylands, in the rural wooded hills of the northwestern corner of the state, retains the aura of the grand estate that it once was. When it was designated the New Jersey State Botanical Garden in 1984, Governor Thomas H. Kean noted that the gardens "hold a treasure of rare and exotic specimens for scores of plant collectors and botanists." How this remote mountaintop property became such a horticultural showplace is the story of two men who owned and developed the land one after the other for over sixty years. Both were successful New Yorkers, one a lawyer and the other a banker, both were trustees of the fledgling New York Botanical Garden and both had bold vision and a passion for landscape.

Above: Colocasia and parrot-feather fill the small grotto pool.

Opposite: Ferrucchio Vitale's formal Italianate terraces extend from the house.

In 1891 Francis Lynde Stetson, a corporate lawyer who specialized in railway litigation and who was personal counsel to J. P. Morgan, bought the property in the Ramapo Mountains and, over time, assembled a group of farms into an 1,100-acre estate. He then hired Samuel F. Parsons Jr. to lay out the grounds. Parsons was an inspired choice. As a protégé of Calvert Vaux, who had designed the Greensward plan for Central Park along with Frederick Law Olmsted, Parsons brought a naturalistic design to Skylands Farm, building twenty-eight miles of roadways that wound through the property, offering visitors carefully framed vistas of the picturesque landscape of mountain outcroppings, spring-fed reservoirs, and farmland. Thousands of roses were planted, along with groves of pine, spruce, and hemlock. A fashionable architect, Alfred Hopkins, was hired to design all of the farm buildings. Skylands became a self-sustaining estate, with its 250 acres of farmland supporting acres of crops, and large chicken houses, a smokehouse, and a dairy contributing to the larder. For the many weekend guests, there were plenty of recreational opportunities, with a tennis court and a nine-hole golf course surrounding the house. After his visit to Stetson, Andrew Carnegie called it the most beautiful country estate in America.

With Stetson's death, Skylands Farm was sold in 1922 to Clarence McKenzie Lewis, a civil engineer, investment banker, and amateur horticulturist. Lewis tore down the Stetson house and hired John Russell Pope to design a forty-five-room Tudor manor house with

half-timber wings, built of native stone quarried on the property. Lewis particularly interested in the varied landscape at Skylands as a setting for his extensive plant
collection, and he hired Ferrucchio Vitale and his partner Alfred Geiffert, who were
responsible for many of the great estates of the Country House era, to further develop
the grounds.

Vitale had apprenticed with Parsons and his partner George Pentecost when the firm
was drawing up the plans for Skylands, and he understood the value of the existing
landscape. In his turn, Vitale removed the golf course and created a series of formal
gardens and allées within the working fields and orchards around the house. With their
lack of walls or distinct edging, the garden beds were unusual for their time. Adjacent
to the house he designed a classical terraced garden, which retains a feeling of great
enclosure and privacy. An octagonal terrace outside the breakfast room gives on to
a walkway lined with star magnolias backed by sweetbays. At the end of the walk,
wisteria-draped stairs lead down to a water lily pool flanked by beds of azaleas and
farther down to the square-shaped rose garden (now planted with daylilies) and a
peony garden beyond.

Lewis was deeply involved in the design for his property, carefully siting his plants so
they would be displayed in the best possible circumstances. Vistas were also important
to him—the view from every room was considered, as well as the curving lines of the
garden beds that would be seen as he passed by. He was a botanizer above all who took
his greatest pleasure in walking the grounds with fellow plant enthusiasts to show his
newest acquisitions, which might be from Afghanistan or Alaska as easily as from New
Jersey. No expense was spared: to create his bog garden in the woodlands, Lewis had
soil brought specially from the Pine Barrens. Skylands was actually registered as a plant
nursery, and Lewis kept meticulous notes and planting records that he shared with
professional horticulturists here and abroad. For thirty years, Lewis had both the money
and the passion to keep up the horticultural showplace at Skylands, but towards the
end of his life he no longer could. He sold the property to a small college in 1953, which
in turn sold it to the state of New Jersey in 1966.

The past grandeur is still strongly felt at Skylands. There are magnificent specimen
trees near the house, including a hundred-year-old red oak, copper beeches and uncommon conifers that wear their great age very well. A few of Lewis's plant discoveries can
still be seen, including Picea orientalis 'Skylands' and Hydrangea anomala petiolaris
ssp. 'Skylands Giant,' which grows on the house itself. The fringed gentian can still be
hunted in the woods. With limited funds, the garden beds are now filled with lower-
maintenance plants, yet they are laid out where Parsons or Vitale placed them, affording an extraordinary opportunity to experience the work of these two great designers.

Right and below: Mature shrubs and trees shade the moraine garden, which over- looks the open lawns.

Opposite: A cherub graces the corner of the octago- nal terrace, with an allée of sweetbay magnolias (Magnolia virginiana) beyond.

Above: The rhododendron garden looking east toward the Ramapo range.

Left: Flowering dogwood with azaleas and pink columbine in early spring.

Opposite: Japanese primrose along the path through the wildflower garden in late May.

KEN DRUSE AND
LOUIS BAUER GARDEN

If one were searching for garden luminaries in New Jersey one need look no further than Ken Druse and Louis Bauer, who share a garden in the northwestern corner of the state. Druse is one of the most prolific and respected garden writers of his generation, and Bauer, formerly Greenwood's horticulturist, is now the director of horticulture at the renowned Wave Hill in the Bronx. The men admit to being passionate collectors, and their island in the Paulinskill River is a kind of gardener's cabinet of curiosities. In addition to plants most gardeners can identify, like roses, hydrangeas, or hostas (albeit represented by the most recherché varieties), there are hundreds of oddities and rarities. Take trees, for example. There are skinny versions of trees that are usually round, miniature forms of familiar giants, others with leaves that are tubular, twisted, variegated or in colors uncharacteristic of their usual presentation.

The story of the garden began twenty years ago when Druse was looking for a country home for his plants. He had outgrown a Soho rooftop and greenhouse in the 1980s and moved to a Brooklyn backyard. Finding that a bit confining, he looked for a larger property and, with luck, water. When he and Bauer saw a small, ramshackle house perched on the high point of the two-acre island, it was love at first sight. The property had a fast-flowing branch of the river on one side and a slow-moving branch on the other. A pretty, arched stone bridge spanned the small canal that bisected the garden. Even though it was a challenging, shady, damp spot with sandy soil, they were smitten.

Reassured that "it never floods," a claim reinforced by the flood-intolerant tree species already growing on the island, they bought the place. Since then it has suffered a number of natural disasters, the worst being the double assault of Hurricane Irene and Tropical Storm Lee in 2011, which left the garden underwater for five days. When the water finally receded, there was as much as two feet of sand in some areas and a legacy of weed seeds that is still causing problems. Part of the garden was completely gone, and debate continues as to whether it will be restored. But the core and many fascinating plants endure, including most of the cherished trees.

Above: Homemade Wave Hill chairs, adapted from a Gerrit Rietveld design.

Opposite: Narrow columnar boxwood (Buxus sempervirens 'Graham Blandy') punctuate the gravel terrace and garden, which is filled with rare and unusual plants. The *faux-bois* plant stand supports a pot filled with pitcher plants (Sarracenia).

Above: Japanese maple (Acer palmatum), one of a number of specimen trees.

Clearing the brush and overgrowth from the middle of the island in the early days had revealed a trove of specimen trees laid out in a circle around a central greensward. The trees probably date from the late nineteenth century and include a magnificent 130-year-old red-leafed Japanese maple (Acer palmatum), a Japanese white cedar (Chamaecyparis pisifera), an ash, and a saucer magnolia (M. x soulangeiana). The open lawn is an important breathing space and change of scale in a garden of so many specimens.

Druse and Bauer accentuated the circle by digging crescent-shaped shrub and perennial borders in front of the trees and interspersing some of their most precious specimens: columnar 'Newton Sentry' sugar maples. These extremely rare trees were propagated from mutated growth found on an old tree in the cemetery in Newton, Massachusetts, in 1898. When Druse located some small trees in a nursery after years of searching, he abandoned his principle of "one of each" and bought seven. After twenty years, the narrow trees have woven themselves into the tapestry of the existing giants, creating a dense and colorful foliage screen around the greensward.

Druse and Bauer clearly find it very hard to resist any plant they take a fancy to. For years Druse would visit Northern California and return with boxes of cuttings and many plants that were hardy but unavailable in the northeast. They spent the year before they moved to the island amassing specimens. The gravel garden, now the heart of the collection, began as a nursery bed. The style of this planting is eclectic, to say the least, with one of each kind of plant. The planted area is backed by a seventy-foot-long stone wall that is covered for most of the growing season by foliage. There are a number of fastigiate boxwoods (Buxus sempervirens 'Graham Blandy') that make a strong design statement on the edge of this garden, carrying the eye to the sod-covered arched stone bridge. Although it is easy to assume that these narrow evergreens were bought for just that purpose, in fact Druse had acquired them and held them in pots for a number of years while he tried to find a place for them.

There is also an exquisite garden of variegated plants that began as one of Druse's "splinter nurseries," where white and green variegated plants were placed until they found permanent homes. The plants looked terrific together, dominated by a magnificent variegated Korean dogwood (Cornus kousa 'Wolf Eyes'), and what Druse calls the "cloud bed" was born. Foliage is paramount in this garden, which is in shade for most of the day.

It is impossible to walk around the garden and not fall into the thrall of plant obsession. Druse and Bauer know each plant as an individual—its name, its origin, its likes and dislikes, quirks, strengths and weaknesses. This is not a place to stand back and observe from afar; it is a highly detailed garden that rewards a close reading of its many fascinating characters.

Above: Four of the seven fastigiate Newton Sentry maples (Acer saccharum 'Newton Sentry'). The shrubs are Hydrangea paniculata 'Brussels Lace' (right) and Viburnum plicatum 'Newport' (left).

Overleaf: The tree canopy is just as varied as the rest of the garden. A Korean Dogwood (Cornus kousa) 'Wolf Eyes' stands to the left of the sod-covered stone bridge.

GARDEN IN NORTHERN NEW JERSEY

The day their youngest child graduated from high school in 1983, the owners of this rural forty-acre property moved full-time to what had been their summer home. The organic vegetable garden that they had started in the late 1960s had been enough to maintain when they were only gardening in the summer, but as soon as they had settled in and built an addition to the original farmhouse, they hired a landscape architect to design more gardens. They have been gardening ever since.

In the process, one of the owners became a garden designer herself, having collaborated on laying out many of the early flower beds, as well as the pergola and hedges in front of the house. She also extended her early interest in organic gardening by learning how to landscape sustainably with the best techniques for soil and lawn maintenance. (Her secret is plenty of manure and compost supplemented by only natural products.) The soil is mostly clay and hardpan, which means that every plant goes in with an extra foot of leaf mold or compost. Since the property is on a limestone ridge, where the soil pH is approximately 7, plants like hellebores and clematis can easily be grown, but it is far more challenging to raise the more traditional woodland plants like rhododendron or azalea.

Above: In the organic vegetable garden, marigolds edge the herb box containing different varieties of basil.

Opposite: The parterre garden near the house, with a sea of forget-me-nots and lady's mantle in early spring.

The owner's hand can be seen throughout the property, where her knowledge of plants and a natural design sense has led her to create a landscape with many different moods, from the welcoming flower-filled beds near the house to the romantic hillside planted for spring with an eye-popping moment when the twenty-five Sargent crabapple 'Tina' bloom. She has been particularly inspired by the work of women garden designers from the past, among them Beatrix Farrand, especially as seen at Dumbarton Oaks. There, the formal gardens around the house give way to outer rings of less formal gardens and plantings until the landscape finally merges with the woodlands. Here, in this garden, stone pathways circle the house and lead one invitingly around corners; stone steps lead out to the woodland gardens that are spread down the hillside to the lake below, with its dramatic, man-made waterfall.

Above: A weeping Katsura is underplanted with hakonechloa.

Opposite, above: The gazebo at the edge of the woodland is draped with sweet clematis.

Opposite, below left: Decorative architectural fragments are used throughout the garden, such as this nineteenth-century iron fencing.

Opposite, below right: Clematis montana billows alongside the house, echoed by the deeper tones of the emerging foliage of the smoketree.

Left, above: An unusual yellow-flowering barberry (Berberis prattii) alongside mossy steps.

Left, below: Spikes of camassia hover above the purple-flowered dusky cranesbill (Geranium phaeum 'Mourning Widow').

Opposite: In the woodlands, a statue of Poseidon looks out over the lake.

Overleaf: White flowering crabapples (Malus sargentii 'Tina') light up the woodland edge in early May.

LAURELWOOD ARBORETUM

WAYNE

For most of us Laurelwood is a revelation—thirty acres of naturalistic planting that features almost 500 choice rhododendrons and azaleas. For connoisseurs, Laurelwood is hallowed ground, filled with exceptional hybrids and historically important varieties. But amateurs and specialists alike can appreciate the way each specimen is lovingly woven into a tapestry of plants and looks completely at home on the sloping hillsides. There was a refined color sense orchestrating this, one that has created a pleasingly pastel ambiance enlivened by the liberal use of white flowers and moments of vivid color. It is clearly the work of a gardener of discrimination, taste, and refinement, which is an excellent description of Dorothy Knippenberg, Laurelwood's creator and still, almost eight years after her death, its guiding spirit.

Knippenberg and her husband, John, bought the thirty acres of woodland across the street from their home in Pines Lake in the 1930s. Its topography was particular: two parallel ridges covered with oak, hickory, and maple interspersed with huge hemlocks. With declining northern faces, the ridges were an ideal configuration for growing ericaceous plants, so when Dorothy Knippenberg started to garden, this was the natural plant palette. She quickly developed a keen interest in rhododendron and azalea in particular, and became a noted hybridizer. Eventually she established a commercial nursery that she called Laurelwood Gardens.

Dorothy Knippenberg, who had attended Pratt Institute in Brooklyn, was a painter at heart. She made her rock and display gardens by thinning the woodland and installing a wide variety of specimens—in "drifts and sweeps," as she used to say. The microclimates created from the differing elevation of ridge and valley provided the opportunity to put together many different garden vignettes. At the higher elevations large plantings of rhododendron and azalea, with bulbs underneath, fill the forest understory, while along the stream banks intricate patterns of plants enjoy the humidity and shelter at the foot of the hills. Fifty years of gardening made Knippenberg tremendously knowledgeable, and each plant in her display gardens is a carefully chosen gem, installed to make it look its best in a natural setting.

Above: Dorothy Knippenberg used pops of vivid color deliberately to call attention to a particular composition.

Opposite: Hundreds of rare rhododendrons and azaleas are displayed in the north-facing woodland.

Overleaf: The extensive displays of azaleas are laid out naturalistically.

John Knippenberg died in 1994, but Dorothy continued to plan for the future and work in her garden. Until well into her nineties, she would walk the comfortable gravel paths and roads with pen and paper in hand, making notes and refining ideas, her keen eye seeing things that her companions couldn't. She had long before decided that she wanted the garden to give pleasure to future generations, foreseeing the time when Pines Lake would become a completely suburban community and thirty acres of gardened woodland would be a precious refuge. She gave Laurelwood to the town of Wayne, and she and a group of friends set up FOLA (Friends of Laurelwood Arboretum) to ensure that the garden would be preserved.

Above: Comfortably wide gravel paths parallel the ridge-lines and the valley floor.

Opposite: Knippenberg believed in creating drifts and sweeps of plants, like this ajuga flowing through the woodland.

Left: The microclimate is ideal for rhododendrons, which have thrived at Laurelwood for sixty years.

Opposite: Knippenberg used white and pale colors to illuminate the woods.

Right and opposite: An intricate mix of evergreen, broad-leaf evergreen, and deciduous shrubs, combined with perennials and bulbs, creates highly textured moments along the banks of the stream as it flows toward the ponds.

Overleaf: The tight planting of the stream banks gives way to the calm of the small lakes.

PRESBY MEMORIAL IRIS GARDENS

UPPER MONTCLAIR

From mid-May through early June, vivid streamers of more than 14,000 iris in all colors of the rainbow unfurl at the base of Mountainside Park. It is one of the high points in the New Jersey garden year, a closely watched annual event that has its own live webcam so that the progress of the blooms can be tracked. Although from a distance the long, narrow garden beds appear like a blur of color, in fact at close quarters each individual iris is shown to perfection, revealing its own particular personality.

Now the largest public iris garden in the country, Presby has survived despite all odds. The garden owes its existence to Barbara Walther, who lived next door to the large tract of land that became Mountainside Park. In 1926 she was asked to spearhead an effort to establish a garden there in honor of Frank Presby, a prominent local businessman. She agreed, and she watched over the garden for the next fifty years. In addition to his deep involvement in civic affairs, Presby had been a serious iris gardener and collector, so Walther and her group of friends focused the small memorial garden on his favorite plant. They collected iris from Presby's own garden and from others in Montclair, from hybridizers all over the world, as well as heirloom iris from the garden of John Caspar Wister, who was the biggest name in American horticulture at the time and who helped lay out the original garden.

Opposite: Long beds packed with iris extend as far as the eye can see.

Above: In the foreground, Bon Appetit, with Rodeo Girl behind.

What began as a modest effort grew more and more extensive until now there are twenty-six long ribbons of beds and 100,000 blooms. Walther expected that visitors would be thrilled to see the newest of the new iris varieties, but in fact the public is drawn to the old-fashioned varieties. They remember the iris that their grandmother or mother grew, and it is this nostalgia for gardens long past that keeps visitors returning to Presby.

Although gardeners will say that iris are easy to cultivate, the display gardens here require high maintenance to keep the plants healthy. In April, the Presby gardeners and volunteers enrich the beds with a top-dressing of compost; beginning in October, they cut down all the foliage; and in December they spread salt hay covered by blueberry netting to serve as a winter blanket. No chemical pesticides or herbicides are ever used. In addition, they dig up and divide the iris rhizomes every two or three years, which gives

Above: The beds are marked with numbers so that they can be compared and judged each year.

Opposite: Barbara Walther's house is now the headquarters for the Citizens Committee of the Presby Memorial Iris Gardens.

the Citizens Committee the chance to offer the rhizomes for sale, raising funds to keep the garden going.

Iris lend themselves to hybridization and, just as John Caspar Wister had once predicted, Presby serves as an invaluable gene pool for hybridizers, who continue to share new introductions, ensuring that the collection thrives and flourishes. Iris with ruffles and frills, iris with riotous color combinations, iris with unusual veining, they are all here and more, astonishing the eye and reminding us of the generations of gardeners before us.

VAN VLECK HOUSE AND GARDENS

MONTCLAIR

Set in a neighborhood of spacious suburban houses, the Van Vleck residence stands out immediately for the elegant simplicity of its limestone facade. But it is the fifty-foot-tall Magnolia grandiflora 'Edith Bogue' beside the house that truly marks this as an unusual place. Miss Bogue gave the tree to Howard Van Vleck, the last family member to live on the estate. An ardent horticulturist, Howard spent fifty years developing his gardens with unusual specimens and, most especially, practicing his passion for hybridizing rhododendrons.

Three generations of Van Vlecks lived here, beginning with Joseph Van Vleck, who moved his wife and ten children from Brooklyn to a large Victorian house on Upper Mountain Road in 1872. Almost immediately, Van Vleck began to transform the property from a working farm and orchard into a landscaped estate. Only twelve miles from Manhattan yet still rural, Montclair was just becoming a desirable suburb, with its burgeoning rail service and advantageous location on the eastward side of the First Watchung Mountain affording excellent views of the city skyline.

The Van Vlecks became a family of architects, and in 1916 Joseph Van Vleck Jr. designed a handsome Italianate villa that his son, Howard, also an architect, moved into in 1939. Joseph Jr. laid out a symmetrical garden behind the house to match its classical architecture. The Italianate "green garden" emphasized foliage and the subtle contrast of different shades of green.

When Howard Van Vleck moved into the house, he set to work changing the gardens into less formal, low-maintenance plantings that would suit a family with four young children and also reflected his own ideas about color, texture, and form. Where there had once been only hostas and columnar junipers in narrow parallel beds, Van Vleck experimented, planting a blend of colorful perennials against a sea of white, punctuated by high-bush blueberries and deep pink Mollis hybrid azaleas. During the Depression, he gave up his architecture practice, explaining to friends that other people needed the work more than he did, and he concentrated on his interest in horticulture. Howard Van Vleck grew and propagated a wide range of plants, many of which he shared with his neighbors. He was particularly focused on creating a clear-yellow flowering rhododendron, and several of his

Above: Bulbs are tucked naturalistically into the shrub beds.

Opposite: The garden peaks in early spring when the many rhododendrons and tree peonies bloom.

Chinese wisteria, dating from 1939, is draped over the courtyard on the back of the house.

hybrids, which he named for members of his family, can still be seen in the gardens. The glory of the house is the pair of Chinese wisteria vines that he planted in 1939 to shade the south-facing courtyard from the afternoon sun—one vine is planted to curl clockwise; the other counter-clockwise.

When Howard Van Vleck died in 1992, his family left the estate to the Montclair Foundation to be used as a public garden, knowing that it was their father's wish to continue to share the garden with friends and neighbors, just as he had shared cuttings and plants all his life. The garden has evolved into a lively community resource, yet there have been few changes made to the landscape. The spirit of a superb plantsman and collector still exists throughout the grounds, where one can walk narrow paths leading to informal glades rimmed with spring-flowering trees and shrubs, many of which were begun from Howard Van Vleck's own cuttings and are now of a venerable size.

SILAS MOUNTSIER AND GRAEME HARDIE GARDENS

NUTLEY

Facing each other across a quiet hilly street in very proper Nutley are two gardens that challenge the notion that the suburbs are not a place to find horticultural and design pyrotechnics. They are products of a fruitful collaboration and friendship between the plantsman and garden designer Richard Hartlage, and the homeowners Silas Mountsier and Graeme Hardie, a three-way conversation that keeps these gardens looking fresh and vital.

Silas Mountsier, a retired banker, is a native. Except for a short spell in New York City ("I didn't like the life.") he has lived in Nutley his entire life. South African Graeme Hardie has lived many places, including North Carolina, where he encountered Richard Hartlage, then a young horticulture graduate. Mountsier and Hardie met in 1989, and it was Hardie who brought Hartlage to Nutley in the early 1990s to help Mountsier renovate his garden, a half-acre overwhelmed with rhododendrons. Hartlage drew up a plan that complemented the blue-green Dutch-colonial house, taking as a departure a round terrace installed in the 1960s. The mostly green garden highlighted Mountsier's growing sculpture collection and also created outdoor spaces to allow Mountsier and Hardie to entertain in the garden. But that was only the beginning.

Twenty years on, the garden has been substantially enlarged, as Mountsier was able to purchase neighboring properties. The collaboration continues. Hartlage has described the garden as "bold and broad," which it is—an abstract painting in three dimensions, with clean, curving lines intersecting with straight ones, and sharp verticals punctuating the space along with well-chosen plants. Now more than two acres, the garden is still predominantly green with substantial plant groupings and occasional assertive color. Each plant group is carefully delineated—as Hardie explains, no "bleeding between plants"—which leads to some great graphic moments. And, because the same clarity of outline applies in the vertical dimension, with hornbeam columns punctuating the garden, there are many memorable compositions that use

Above and opposite: Among the sculptures installed in the Mountsier garden are the Jersey cow by English artist Geraldine Knight and an abstract figure by Lennard Cave.

59

a shifting arrangement of the uprights, the horizontal lines and the many different greens to great advantage.

A visitor is always aware of the geometry, yet the whole is never visible on the ground. Only from a viewing platform eight feet in the air does the whole complex puzzle resolve itself.

Hartlage says that he designed the garden as a crucible for Mountsier's art: years of befriending artists has resulted in a diverse collection, each piece set off to advantage in its own setting. The other notable feature is the careful selection of plant varieties in the garden—not only are they all choice specimens but they provide interest all through the year, from the sea of hellebores through the magnolias, cherries, and dogwoods, through to the autumn glory of the grasses and maples.

The design gestures become bolder farther from the house. The strongest, most contemporary moment is a wide lawn bounded by a semicircular berm interrupted by rectangular concrete walls set at differing angles. The berm is planted with different tints of the Japanese grass hakonechloa, which has a soft waving habit that sways gently in the slightest breeze and in mass can seem almost alive. The colors progress in bands from strong green through bright yellow —"a rainbow of grasses," as Hartlage describes it. The effect is stunning, as well as supremely architectural, controlled, and neat.

Opposite, from top left: Pond and terrace designed by Richard Hartlage; lawns are inserted between intensively planted and designed sections of the garden; Liriope mound called "Mount Sier."

Overleaf: The dramatic berm punctuated by concrete walls at different angles is planted with several varieties of hakonechloa.

Right and below: A triangular curved roof by artist Tim Abbot shelters a seating area. Its shape is echoed in the caladium inserts that provide a graphic contrast to the ground cover.

Opposite: A billowing climbing hydrangea softens the brick wall, whose rectilinear piers are echoed by the euonymus column behind.

Above and opposite: White-flowering cherries bloom in early spring when the greenhouse is still full of overwintering plants. The greenhouse is emptied out in the summer as plants are distributed around the garden.

Opposite: Japanese maples underplanted with a fine show of hellebores.

Above, left: The view of Silas Mountsier's house from the street. The vivid quince is a harbinger of spring.

Above, right: Daffodils catch the early morning light.

Across the street, Graeme Hardie's garden is at the other end of the spectrum. When he renovated his trim 1880s house, he turned to Hartlage to design the landscape. The front of the house is formally laid out with plants that complement the sedate gray with maroon-brown trim, giving no indication of what is going to happen in the back yard. Hartlage has given Hardie plenty of architecture, including a cleverly configured path system that makes the most of the small space. But the real impact is the planting. Hardie likes a jungle, and that's what he has, a vivid explosion of color and tropical leaf form that's as exuberant and vivid as he is himself.

The garden is completely enclosed by high walls, painted three colors of bright blue, and the garage, which faces the house and is camouflaged with a colonnade to make it look like a cottage. Three different terraces make the most of the five-foot elevation change in the garden, and the textures of the paths help differentiate parts of the journey through the garden.

The garden looks different every year, as the mix of bromeliads, solanum, coleus, begonia, caladium, philodendron, ginger, and other assorted tropicals changes. The garden does have some permanent plantings: columns of variegated euonymus march through the middle; a dark-leaved smokebush echoes the color of the dusky rubber plant at the bottom. In the summer, tall daylilies poke their yellow heads up though the tropical foliage. But the overall character comes from the jungle.

Above: Precise planting in color-ways that match Graeme Hardie's house give no hint of the mood of the garden behind.

Opposite: Shaped boxwood barely contains the exuberant display of hosta, philodendron, coleus, and impatiens.

Right and opposite: The surprising blue of the walls sets a festive tone. Coleus in many patterns is a staple of the summer garden. By midsummer the pots are overflowing, and the plantings almost overwhelm the sculpture.

Overleaf: Nicolas Moreton's *Suckle Me To My Breast*.

MARA SEIBERT AND
LENORE AND BOB RICE GARDENS

SHORT HILLS

Environmentalists and urban planners have been lobbying for years for a new approach to the area between the house and the street, but homeowners are loathe to give up the iconic front lawn and its associations with prosperity. The landscape architect Richard Hartlage has designed two very different modern gardens for his friends Mara Seibert and Lenore Rice that do away with the front lawns and complement traditional architecture at the same time.

Seibert and Rice are partners in their eponymous firm, which imports high-quality Italian terra-cotta pots. They live in Short Hills, one of the nation's earliest planned communities, and each has a house in the historic district that beautifully represents the eras when they were built. Seibert's stone Arts and Crafts–inspired house dates to 1907. Her property is adjacent to the Short Hills Country Club, and she wanted a park-like feel for the extensive back garden. Seibert had known Richard Hartlage for more than a decade when he invited her to dinner with Silas Mountsier and Graeme Hardie. She was so struck with the architectural tone Hartlage had set in Mountsier's garden that she asked him to take a look at hers.

Above: Terra-cotta pots, such as this one planted with succulents, are found throughout the garden.

Opposite: An overgrown terrace has been reimagined as an elegant gravel garden with curving boxwood hedges.

The result is a fresh take on the front yard and a graceful Olmstedian back garden. In order to reconfigure the front, two huge out-of-scale spruce had to come down. The neighbors were understandably nervous. Then, when the tiny plugs of grass plants went in, there was general consternation. Now, most agree that it's a dramatic contemporary statement that perfectly sets off the multicolored stone of the house. The clearly defined shapes of the front beds along the street are planted with dark green liriope (Liriope spicata), backed by a bed of plumed fountain grass (Pennisetum alopecuroides 'Cassian') in front of a hedge of leather-leaf viburnum. In contrast, the foundation planting has a straight edge and is filled with the airy seedheads of a switchgrass (Panicum virgatum). This might seem to be a monochromatic planting, but, in fact, the colors of the large grasses change from light green in the spring to a rich, tawny brown in the fall.

Above: Lilyturf (Liriope spicata) and grasses (Pennisetum alopecuroides 'Cassian') were a bold choice for the front of the house.

Opposite: Rustic steps from the shady gravel garden lead to the wide lawn of the back garden, whose traditional planting contrasts with the contemporary feel of the front of the house.

In the backyard, the job was mostly editing and opening up the spaces. A line of Pee Gee hydrangeas in huge Seibert and Rice pots edges the generous terrace. In doing the work, Seibert discovered an overgrown terrace area overlooking the neighboring pond, which Hartlage spruced up with two sinuous boxwood hedges facing each other across a gravel courtyard.

Lenore and Bob Rice's garden couldn't be more different. Set on a very steep hill, the house is one of a group of Tudor cottages built in the 1920s. The Rices had done a little landscaping, but several downed trees had changed the configuration of the space. Inspired by a visit to Graeme Hardie's, where Hartlage had put a lot of garden into a small space, they asked him to look at their backyard. Initially, they had thought that he might just rework the small, flat area, but in the end he redesigned the entire space, making a woodland path and more small terraces on the hill that rises steeply behind the house, exponentially expanding the livable area.

The back of the house was such a success that when Hartlage suggested that the Rices get rid of the grass in their front yard and replace it with a garden, they agreed. The front is equally steep, and Hartlage installed a cottage garden for the twenty-first century, replacing the lawn with ground-hugging shrubs and with perennials and grasses that tumble down the hill in not quite wild abandon. A brilliant bulb display in the spring is replaced by burgeoning perennials in a show that continues until the last of fall's asters and grasses.

Opposite and above: This modern take on a traditional cottage garden is vibrant from early spring to late fall. Here, bluebeard (caryopteris), asters, grasses and rudbeckia create a captivating fall garden.

Above, left: Clipped boxwood lines the walkway to the front door, contrasting with the exuberant flowers and grasses.

Above, right: Colocasia in a tall Seibert and Rice pot, at the foot of stairs to the woodland hillside.

Opposite: Gourds hang from the backyard arbor.

GREENWOOD GARDENS

SHORT HILLS

Joseph Day was the most successful real estate auctioneer of his era, said to have sold off half of the Bronx and Queens and large parts of Westchester and Northern New Jersey. He was also a real character: a 1933 *New Yorker* profile described him as "a man of great gusto and personality" and, if photographs are to be believed, his garden, Pleasant Days, set on the western ridge of the Watchung Mountains, had similar qualities. The architect, William Whetten Renwick (he had worked for his uncle James Renwick Jr., the architect of St. Patrick's Cathedral in Manhattan), designed an exuberant house and elaborate garden for Day that was influenced by both Italian tradition and the Arts and Crafts movement. Many of the design ideas in the Day garden seem to be expanded versions of things Renwick had first done in his own garden, a stone's throw from Pleasant Days. Renwick, who had practiced as an ecclesiastical architect, embraced both the newest technology and the oldest crafts, especially indigenous American art pottery and tile work. The gardens, like the house, were heavily ornamented.

The Day gardens, constructed between 1912 and 1929, consisted of a series of lavishly planted terraces, descending from the large house, which was built by the Guastavino Fireproof Construction Company. A series of interlocking terraces stepped down from the south facade. The first level was a simple surround for the house; the next featured a wading pool and fountain and a croquet lawn; and, at the bottom of the hill, the lowest terrace was the fanciful "Garden of the Gods," which consisted of a basin with another fountain, surrounded by an arbor and many statues. A dramatic cascade tumbled down from the east facade where there was a heavily decorated two-story teahouse. Rock gardens, statuary, greenhouses, a summerhouse, a tennis pavilion, many pergolas, a huge vegetable garden, cottages, stables, and a nine-hole golf course completed the estate. The Arts and Crafts influence can be seen in the materials used throughout the gardens, which were not quite rustic but somewhat coarse, colorful, and textured. The chunky structures were made of multicolored stone and decorated inside and out with colorful glazed Rookwood tiles, which were also used in garden niches. An extensive system of paths was made from specially designed exposed aggregate pavers, cutting-edge technology at the time that imparted a rough texture that the designers could then shape to fit the paths. The planting was seasonal and bright.

Above: The hedge of gold-leaved Spiraea thunbergii 'Ogon' provides a vibrant cross axis.

Opposite: The allée of London plane trees (Platanus x acerifolia) beside the entrance drive was one of several allées planted by the Blanchards.

Day's real estate empire declined after the Depression, and he died in 1944. Pleasant Days was acquired in 1949 by Peter P. Blanchard Jr., who married Adelaide Childs Frick the following year. The Blanchards had a more Eurocentric aesthetic, reinforced over the years by frequent travel. They renamed the property Greenwoods and replaced the flamboyant house with a prim Georgian brick structure. Retaining the Day-era buildings, terracing, and ornamentation (except some of the pergolas), they used evergreens to trace an Italianate overlay upon the garden. The new plantings emphasized views and axes. They planted allées of sycamore, pine, and spruce and hedges of hemlock, yew, and boxwood. The calming order of axis and cross axis, the unifying darker color of the evergreen architecture, and the hillsides of boxwood complemented the earthy styling of the Arts and Crafts elements of the earlier era. Peter Blanchard, who was widowed in 1956, lavished time and attention on the garden, realizing perhaps that with this curious hybridization of style and aesthetics a unique garden voice had emerged.

Blanchard stipulated in his will that the property be given to a conservation organization after his death. With support from the Garden Conservancy, his son, Peter, and his wife, Sofia, founded Greenwood Gardens in 2003 for this purpose, turning the property into a public garden. After ten years of planning, fundraising, and restoration work, which included rebuilding the terrace in front of the house and modernizing all the utilities, the garden reopened in April 2013. Louis Bauer directed the work of cutting back and replanting hedges, pruning trees, and opening up sight lines, and at the same time he quietly built a horticultural showplace. He used a huge plant "vocabulary" and the garden he created at Greenwood is like a richly worded book, immensely enjoyable, all the more so when at times you have to refer to the dictionary.

For the team that runs Greenwood and for its growing numbers of visitors, the garden has a distinctive voice. This is partly due to the amalgam of styles that distinguishes it from other historic gardens and increasingly to its erudite horticulture. But the key factor is sanctuary. The original one hundred acres of the Day property have been reduced to twenty-eight, but Greenwood is surrounded on three sides by the South Mountain Reservation and, on the fourth, by Short Hills Park. Despite the suburban location, a panoramic view from the house terrace still reveals nothing but forest, meadow, and sky.

Above: The very early blooming Edgeworthia chrysantha has a choice spot in front of the tea house.

Opposite: Limestone chess figures, bought by the Blanchards, line a pathway of exposed aggregate pavers that were specially made for the Day garden.

Left: The Arts and Crafts influence can be seen in the Rookwood tiles in the niche in the wall of the reflecting pool terrace.

Opposite: The silver sheen of the bluebeard (Caryopteris divaricata 'White Mist') is echoed by artemisia and lamb's ears.

Overleaf: The former reflecting pool is planted with water lovers, including glaucous sedge (Carex flacca 'Blue Zinger') and several different iris, as well as cattails (Typha latifolia 'Variegata') and lingonberry (Vaccinium vitis-idaea).

REEVES-REED ARBORETUM

SUMMIT

In the late nineteenth century, Summit was a popular destination for wealthy families looking to escape New York City. With its position on top of the Second Watchung Ridge, Summit offered cool breezes and fresh air. One of the wealthy businessmen drawn there was John Hornor Wisner, who built a Colonial Revival house for his family in 1889 that he named The Clearing, and, in a move that ensured his imprint on the property, hired Calvert Vaux to draw up a landscape plan.

Vaux's proposal drew on the Greensward Plan that he and Frederick Law Olmsted had produced for Central Park in New York City. The view from the house was over the open space of the dells, with vistas carved out of the forest— the Wisners could see as far as New York City. Mrs. Wisner planted the first groups of daffodils, an effort that would be added to many times over by the families that followed. In 1916, after their children were grown, the Wisners sold the house and moved back to the city. The next owners, Richard and Susie Reeves, lived at The Clearing for fifty years; it was they who added the decorative flower gardens.

Above and opposite: Thousands of narcissus line the path and fill the hillside in April.

Susie Graham Reeves was an excellent hands-on gardener, and in 1924 she hired Ellen Biddle Shipman, whose plans included gardens, terraces, and a swimming pool. Wary of the considerable maintenance costs involved, Mrs. Reeves looked elsewhere and hired Carl Pilat instead. Having been the landscape architect for the New York City parks department, Pilat understood how important it was to preserve Vaux's plan, but he also chose to incorporate some of Shipman's ideas with his own, siting a terrace and a series of new garden rooms in a way that did not interfere with Vaux's naturalistic open space. The most important addition was a formal rose garden, where Mrs. Reeves grew her prize-winning roses. In addition, Mrs. Reeves planted thousands of daffodils in the curve of the glacial bowl in the back of the house. Now, more than 40,000 daffodils bloom each April, followed by a meadow planting of late-summer Joe-Pye weed, ironweed, cone-flower, and goldenrod.

Landscapes undergo changes over time, and at Reeves-Reed the layers of changes, the shifts in design intention, are still very visible. Beside the Vaux design and the Shipman-Pilat gardens is a more recent mandala-patterned herb garden that was added by Charles

Above: Tom Holmes's sculpture *Inner Strength* stands in the formal garden area where crabapples bloom in early spring.

Opposite: In April, magnolias begin to unfurl their blooms at the edge of the field of narcissus.

L. Reed and his wife, Ann, who was a niece of Susie Reeves. During their tenure in the late 1960s, they also created trails through the woodlands so they could see the spring-blooming Jack-in-the-pulpit, mayapple, and lady slippers. In 1974, the property was sold to the city of Summit to preserve open space for the community, and since then staff and many volunteers have worked to maintain the gardens to a high level. More recently, the staff at Reeves-Reed has installed a rotating sculpture exhibit that attracts many visitors and enlivens the gardens from June to October. This would most certainly have pleased Susie Reeves, who enjoyed sharing her garden and is said to have put a welcome sign out on the road every spring so that neighbors would come in and see the daffodils put on their April show.

KENNELSTON COTTAGE

FAR HILLS

Spectacular flower displays and carefully chosen garden ornaments characterize this garden, which wraps around a Tudor-style house extensively renovated by Mott Schmidt in the 1940s. The architect's traditional elegance is echoed in a series of immaculate, formal garden rooms decorated with urns, planters, and statues. Mature trees, perfectly cared for, dot the grounds.

When Gates and Mary Ellen Hawn moved to the thirty-acre property in 1995, they engaged landscape architect Brian Bosenberg to lay out gardens. Mindful of the deer problem, he designed a series of terraces hugging the southern and western facades and a partially enclosed enfilade of gardens to the west. This is linked to the house by an intimate court-yard garden and a grassed allée, terminating in a decorative iron gate and stone stairs leading down to the enfilade. Beside the courtyard is a recently rebuilt garden terrace featuring a lozenge-shaped pool with a small, whimsical fountain.

The suite of gardens includes a two-chambered, trellis-enclosed ornamental potager. The assertive decorative trellis sets the tone for the parterres, which are planted with a mix of well-behaved vegetables and ornamentals; gravel walkways and neat brick edging reinforce the traditional tone of the gardens. Each section has a piece of antique statuary or an urn as a focal point. The formality is counterbalanced by the homey, tra-ditional hollyhocks, which flower magnificently against the trellis walls in midsummer. A stone path leads from the potager to the azalea circle, which in turn leads to the closely planted approach to the secret garden. A small entrance pavilion is stylistically related to the potager trellis, but with its strong verticals and steeply pitched roofline, quite distinct. It marks the transition to the shady secret garden, planted within the ruins of an old barn and protected with more sturdy, dark-painted trellis. Here, a parterre with mossy paths, clipped boxwood edging and many astilbe creates a soothing backdrop for a delicate nymph sculpture emerging from a ring of pink spirea.

Mary Ellen Hawn was not a gardener when they bought the house, and she had early help from garden designer Ania Bass. But in acquiring the property she found her calling, and

Opposite and above: Hundreds of purple allium offer a big show in the pool garden, where a few white iris and clematis stand out in contrast.

Overleaf: The snail fountain is one of a group of playful statues installed in the garden.

99

now she is fully in charge. The planting schemes are constantly being tweaked and upgraded. There is a remarkable attention to detail, so a close-up of any part of the garden reveals the same flawless good taste and refined tone as the whole.

Below the house, the swimming pool is surrounded by flower beds. In mid-spring, thousands of purple allium, set off by a few chaste white iris and clematis, make a huge show. Nearby, a border of six different varieties of hydrangea, as well as painted fern and hosta, blooms later in the season.

At the eastern edge of the property is an English glasshouse, originally built to house a few tender plants and now bursting with decorative pots throughout the winter; behind it is a stylized "box-wood" farm, linked to another working but decorative plant nursery/parterre. The boxwood, clipped into squares and circles in neat rows, is an unexpected and playful visual treat.

This garden is never "quiet"—during the growing season, there is always something blooming. But probably the absolute peak of the gardening year is the spectacular rose display. In the terraces by the house and in the trellised enclosures, fences and walls are smothered in fragrant climbers, and classic combinations like New Dawn and purple clematis drape the doorways. The roses suit the English-inflected architecture, and their strong scent and clear, pastel colors, mostly white, blush apricot, and pale pink, add a romantic, fairytale quality to the garden while they are at their zenith.

Above: Further from the house, a relaxed hydrangea hedge camouflages an old stone pile.

Opposite, above: Fancifully clipped boxwood in front of the Victorian greenhouse.

Opposite, below: In May and June roses festoon the terraces around the house.

Above and opposite: The potager is productive as well as decorative. Hollyhocks add an informal note while an old chimney pot makes an elegant plant stand.

Above: Climbing hydrangea draped over a doorway.

Opposite: A nymph emerging from dwarf spiraea in the secret garden.

Overleaf: The approach to the secret garden is closely planted with perennials that do well in light shade, like lady's mantle and hosta.

LEONARD J. BUCK GARDEN

FAR HILLS

There is a point somewhere in mid-April, when the delicate green of the new leaves is just starting to outline the
branches of the trees, creating a chartreuse scrim against
the pale spring sky, and early ephemerals—Erythronium,
Aquilegia canadensis, Phlox divaricata—are peeking from
the dusty brown leaf litter on the forest floor. At that
moment the Leonard J. Buck Garden is unquestionably the
most beautiful place in New Jersey. The rock garden and
woodland plants, many of them rare and unusual, fit seamlessly into their valley setting, and the quiet pleasure of a
stroll becomes an intense immersion into the possibilities
of spring. Never, however, does it seem that this woodland
is anything but a naturally occurring phenomenon. This is
the genius of the garden.

Opposite: Leonard Buck
exposed the rock walls of the
valley and tucked his woodland
and rock garden plants into its
cracks and crevasses.

Above: Delicate erythronium in
the woodland.

In 1937 Leonard Buck, a mining engineer by training and also a plantsman and a trustee
of The New York Botanical Garden, bought the fifty-acre estate that included a dramatic
gorge ninety feet deep and six hundred feet across. The gorge was part of Moggy Hollow,
a glacial relic, with basalt rock ledges and outcroppings. There were other remnants of
geologic activity on the property, which he named Allwood, and he soon began developing plans for a garden that would highlight the unique features of the place. His partner in
the garden was the designer Zenon Schreiber, a Swiss landscape architect with a specialty
in award-winning rock gardens, whose private clients included the Rockefeller family and
President Dwight D. Eisenhower. Schreiber worked on the garden continuously from 1943
to 1953 and thereafter on a project basis. Their collaboration lasted thirty-five years.

Buck and Schreiber painstakingly uncovered rock outcroppings, taking advantage of each
formation's exposure and microclimates to provide the perfect home for woodland and
rock plants and to create subtly different displays. The result is that each outcropping
with its precious specimens seems like a natural happening, so different from constructed
rock garden landscapes with their tufa rocks and perfectly screened gravel.

The Moggy Brook adds the magic to the landscape. Schreiber was known for his massed
planting and sinuous paths and for using water to add life to his designs. At the Buck
garden, the placid brook, spanned here and there by rustic bridges, its banks lined with

elegantly pinned locust logs, expands from time to time to form small ponds. Its meandering progression through the flat valley floor is a perfect counterpoint to the sharp and primeval rock outcroppings of the valley walls.

Buck was a hands-on gardener, and it took up a lot of his time—so much so that at one point his wife threatened that if he cleared one more outcropping she would go to Reno for a divorce. (That outcropping became known as "Reno Rock.") Buck was also very much a part of a vibrant local gardening community, and he was a frequent visitor at Willowwood, home of the Tubbs brothers. And, though he was well known to be averse to publishing pictures of his garden, fearing imitation, he entertained hundreds of garden tours.

Buck died in 1974, and his wife, Helen, gave the garden to Somerset County in 1976. It is considered the crown jewel of the Somerset County park system and has received unusually sensitive and progressive stewardship in the ensuing years. The focus on plantsmanship has been maintained—in fact, for some years one of the horticulturists had an import license to bring in rare plants from Asia.

During a recent restoration the garden was brought up to the original standard or above, complete with the locust logs pegged in to stabilize the stream bed, just as they were in the Buck era. Bridges and benches for the public have been replaced with rustic furniture made by David Robinson, well known for his work restoring the pavilions in Central Park. An effort is being made to extend the bloom season, with fall colors creating another vibrant moment.

The secret of a successful woodland garden is the quality of the light. The canopy is ever-changing: too much light, and the delicate woodland plants die and the picture flattens; too little light, and the dappled shade turns to gloom. The gardeners in charge of the Buck Garden have handled this problem brilliantly, controlling the canopy and the shade as much as possible to preserve that delicate balance and create a truly exceptional garden experience.

Opposite: Locust logs are pegged into the stream banks to stabilize them. The bridges have been rebuilt in a rustic style.

Opposite: Constant attention to the tree canopy assures a dappled light that encourages woodland plants.

Right: Dogwood blooming on the steep sides of the Moggy Hollow ravine. The cleared rock face beneath is alive with spring bloomers.

Above: Rare wake robin trillium (Trillium kurabyashii) (left) and Epimedium (right).

Opposite: Buck was fascinated by the geology of Moggy Hollow, where hard basaltic rock forms the walls of the ravine.

Opposite and above: In spring, color comes from leaf as well as flower, as seen in an unfolding Japanese maple and the early-blooming Japanese spice-bush (Lindera obtusiloba).

Overleaf: Primrose (Primula sieboldii), native columbine (Aquilegia canadensis), moss phlox (Phlox subulata),and Basket of Gold (Alyssum montanum 'Luna') are set off by the black basalt outcropping known as Big Rock.

ELLISTAN

PEAPACK

Traditionally, the Essex County Hunt assembles at Ellistan, a 70-acre farm in the Somerset Hills, before setting off for their Thanksgiving meet. The 1931 house designed by Musgrove Hyde was named for Ellistan Boy, a legendary steeplechaser fatally injured on the property a hundred years ago. The Norman chateau-style house in tan stone with a dark brown roof was built for a family with four polo-playing sons and must have seemed quite severe without the warm, hospitable effect of the gardens that now surround the house.

The transformation started when George Bletsil of Innocenti and Webel drew up a master plan for the property. In the early 1990s Shelby Doggett Mellick working with Hank Slack, by then the owner of the property, took the master plan and added a series of gardens. A terrace at the back of the house was partially enclosed with trellis, which made it feel more protected, and this area was designated the white garden. Its high point is the white wisteria that climbs the interstices between the French doors on the ground floor. To the side of the house a circular pool became the center of an old-fashioned flower garden, with beds surrounding the pool, which was graced with a distinctive lead crane rising elegantly from the center.

When Sarah and Hank Slack married in 1995, Mellick, Hank Slack's cousin as well as landscape designer, handed over the garden to the new bride. Although Sarah Slack was English, she had never gardened. "Shelby handed me a gift," she says now. "The garden has been a great adventure." The adventure began with help from a friend, famed British garden designer Penelope Hobhouse. Building on Mellick's garden, they expanded, refining the borders, adding hedges to make different garden rooms, increasing the flow between gardens and linking the disparate areas with boxwood.

Sarah Slack has taken to gardening, and continues to orchestrate the complex mix of plantings. The mature gardens, resplendent with rose-covered arches, ample hedges, burgeoning perennials—in shades of pinks to wine to blue, with bottom notes of deep purple in the smokebush, heuchera and black-leaved cimicifuga—provide a warm and richly textured counterpoint to the austere lines of the house.

Above: Delicate euphorbia in front of the wisteria on the terrace.

Opposite: Structure and color are evenly balanced, and the palette of blues, pinks and purples is pleasing but not overwhelming.

Above: Trellis encloses the white garden at the back of the house.

Opposite: The somber tones of the house are brightened by the luxuriance of the garden.

Overleaf: The elegantly proportioned and detailed main room of the garden.

DUNWALKE EAST

BEDMINSTER

When diplomat, statesman and financier C. Douglas Dillon built Dunwalke East in 1938, not far from Dunwalke, his father's estate, he commissioned the top practitioners of his era—Mott Schmidt and Innocenti and Webel—to build a house amid the rolling farmland. Both architect and landscape firm were known for their timeless designs using modern methods to achieve a look that was grounded in history and informed by classical tradition. Both relied on symmetry, proportion, and fine craftsmanship to create work that communicated an aura of cultured affluence without ostentation.

Those qualities attracted collectors Dexter and Carol Earle, who bought the house in 1993. Since then, they have worked to complement the classic bones they inherited. This is especially true of the outdoor spaces, which included a series of flower gardens that had been designed for the Dillons by John Charles Smith, a local landscape architect. For instance, inspired by the stone eagles mounted on the gates of Dunwalke, the Earles placed pairs of cast-lead eagles to guard the openings of the garden rooms, and the eagles are now the unofficial mascots at Dunwalke East.

Above: Hundreds of colorful orchids fill the Victorian greenhouse.

Opposite: Antique garden ornaments include an early eighteenth-century Flemish gritstone putto, shaded by a Korean dogwood (Cornus kousa).

Avid collectors of porcelain, antique furniture, and eighteenth- and nineteenth-century painting, the Earles added garden ornaments to their list of interests. A close friendship with the antiques dealer Fred Nadler, who once told the Earles "there's always room for one more thing!" resulted in a varied trove of garden statuary, from the magnificent cast-iron urn that provides an important focal point in the entrance courtyard to the cast-iron and zinc three-tiered fountain in the rose garden. When Nadler died in 2003, the couple turned to the noted garden antiques dealer Barbara Israel, and she found the four early eighteenth-century gritstone putti that add such character to the rose garden.

In addition to a superb collection of garden ornaments, there is something else that sets this garden apart, and that is estate manager Joe Thomas, the third part of the triumvirate that oversees Dunwalke East. A meticulous craftsman, he has replaced overgrown yew hedges with Carol Earle's favorite boxwood. He clips the more than 850 specimens each year, echoing in green the ordered geometry of the hardscape. In addition to the foundation plantings and the magnificent specimen trees, there is a sunken parterre rose garden, on axis with the narrower side of the house and anchored by fully mature Korean dogwoods (Cornus kousa). From the rose garden, which features mostly hybrid teas, there is a wide view across productive fields to a pastoral landscape, recalling large estates in English landscape painting.

Farther from the house is the peony garden for which Dunwalke East is famous. The Earles replaced the original lilac hedge with a low brick wall, added statuary—including the nineteenth-century iron whippets at the entrance—and planted the peonies into boxwood parterres. The peonies, only whites and pinks, spill over their boxwood bases with glorious abandon.

Among other improvements, the Earles have added a discreetly landscaped pool, tucked into the woods so not to disturb the elegant classicism of the house. The most dramatic addition is the greenhouse, which is dedicated to Carol Earle's orchid collection. The Earles have vacationed and owned a house in Hawaii for many years. There, Carol Earle developed an affection for orchids, which she picked up at farmer's markets. When she brought them back to Bedminster, she discovered that Joe Thomas was also passionate about the flowers, and thus collections are made. A small second-hand greenhouse was soon overrun so in 2007 the Earles designed their Messenger glasshouse, which was assembled on site incorporating antique artifacts, including a door from the old Peacock Alley at the Waldorf Astoria. The glasshouse now holds more than 1,000 plants and provides blooming orchids for every room of the house.

Opposite, above: The formality of the rose garden gives way to an open view over the agricultural fields.

Opposite, below: The front courtyard features an elaborate cast-iron urn and a pair of nineteenth-century cast-lead eagles.

Overleaf: Crabapples in early May.

Right and opposite: The peony garden in full bloom in white and tones of pink. The miniature nineteenth-century iron whippets are quite rare.

Overleaf: Stately Korean dogwoods (Cornus kousa) flank the Georgian-style house, designed by Mott Schmidt, seen from the agricultural fields that abut the lawn.

CROSS ESTATE

BERNARDSVILLE

Julia Newbold Cross knew what a great garden was. Her parents, Thomas and Sarah Newbold, had commissioned Beatrix Farrand for their own garden at Bellefield in Hyde Park, New York. So it is not surprising that, in 1931, shortly after buying the 204-acre estate that the Crosses would name Hardscrabble House, Mrs. Cross (who had brought her greenhouse with her when she moved from Morristown) hired the well-regarded society landscape architect Clarence Fowler to assist her in creating gracious gardens of her own.

Mrs. Cross's gardens were installed quite close to the large stone and stucco house, yet nearly invisible thanks to a screen of laurel and rhododendron that was planted

in 1951 for their daughter's wedding and that is now of a magnificent size. Through the gate, a stone pergola draped with climbing hydrangea, sweet autumn clematis, blue and white wisteria, and male kiwi vines overlooks both the sunken, walled garden and the neighboring, more naturalistic garden. Fowler's formal, geometric hardscape is perfectly balanced by the distant view of the Somerset hills.

Mrs. Cross was president of the New York Horticultural Society and a member of the Garden Club of Somerset Hills, along with her neighbors from Willowwood, Henry Tubbs and Dr. Benjamin Blackburn, and the landscape architect Martha Brookes Hutcheson, who became a friend and garden adviser. Flowers grown on the Cross estate by the head gardener, Anthony Sailer, regularly won prizes at the flower shows that were popular at the time. Mrs. Cross's formal garden would have been planted primarily with annuals, chosen for their seasonal color and interest.

After Mrs. Cross's death in 1972, most of the property became part of the Morristown National Historical Park. The gardens languished until 1977, when volunteers of the New Jersey Historical Garden Foundation started a restoration project. Although a pair of waist-high terra-cotta urns still anchored the squares in the upper terrace, almost all of the plants from the Cross era were gone. Replanting the overgrown beds gave the volunteers the opportunity to eliminate the maintenance-heavy annual plantings in favor of a rich and varied palette of perennials and small shrubs. Now the formal garden is a romantic and evocative place, particularly in the spring when the peonies, iris, lilac,

Above: An ancient silver maple on the back lawn, near a recently planted garden lined with boxwood.

Opposite: Flowering almond blooms in a riot of forget-me-nots in the walled garden.

Overleaf: The walled garden in early spring, with forget-me-nots and iris dotting the beds. The urns date from Mrs. Cross's era.

Opposite, above: Nineteen stone columns support the wisteria pergola beside the formal walled garden.

Opposite, below: A weeping redbud, Cercis canadensis 'Covey,' anchors one of the beds in the fern-filled woodland garden.

Right: Columbine and Geranium 'Johnson's Blue' in the fern garden underneath two mature Korean dogwoods (Cornus kousa), planted by Mrs. Cross in the 1930s.

and flowering almond all bloom in a sea of forget-me-nots. In what was once a nursery area alongside the formal garden, the volunteers have created a wild garden, cultivating ferns, mayapple and other native woodland plants underneath redbuds and ancient azaleas, lilac, and enkianthus.

Elsewhere on the property there are trees of a size befitting a landscape that has been tended for over a hundred years. In particular, there is a silver maple on the front lawn, planted in 1905, that is reaching the end of its lifespan yet still strongly anchors the house, a huge copper beech near the wild garden, and a dawn redwood, grown from seeds given to Mrs. Cross by Dr. Blackburn of Willowwood.

Right: Yellow-blooming Jasminum nudiflorum with forget-me-nots.

Opposite: Syringa meyeri 'Palinbin' and Peony lactiflora, one of the old peonies in the walled garden.

WILLOWWOOD ARBORETUM

CHESTER TOWNSHIP

Willowwood is a garden that inspires affection. Although it has a serious collection of rare and unusual specimens, it feels like the home the Tubbs brothers and later their friend Dr. Benjamin Blackburn loved. Remarkably, the garden still reads like a personal expression of the three cultivated gentlemen who tended it.

Situated in a shallow bowl in the Hacklebarney Hills, in a rural pocket of the state, the 130-acre property has been farmed since the 1790s. In 1908 brothers Hal and Robert Tubbs, who were both avid gardeners, discovered it after a yearlong search for a retreat from New York City. When they saw the modest farmhouse with its already venerable outbuildings of local puddingstone, set in what was then open farmland, they bought it immediately.

Hal Tubbs, the elder brother and a talented artist, moved in full time and was soon joined by his parents and sister. Developing the grounds became an ongoing family project. The property, which they renamed Willowwood for the huge willows growing by the brook, was transformed into a "gentleman's farm." Robert Tubbs, who came from the city on weekends, had a collector's passion for woody plants, and he was in touch with a wide circle of the leading plantsmen and plantswomen of his day. Among them was Ernest "Chinese" Wilson, the famous plant hunter and manager of the Arnold Arboretum, who, like many of Robert's correspondents, sent seeds and cuttings, building the framework for the extensive collection of trees at Willowwood today.

Above: The white garden in the rear of the house retains Hal Tubbs's formal layout.

Opposite: The central axis of the cottage garden leads to the front door and is carried through to the formal garden in the rear.

In the 1930s the Tubbs brothers befriended a young botanist and landscape gardener named Benjamin Blackburn, who would often visit them at the farm. When Blackburn returned from miiitary service after World War II, he came to live at Willowwood with Hal Tubbs, whose parents and siblings had died. Tubbs encouraged Blackburn to pursue his doctorate at Rutgers and start what would become a long and productive career, authoring three books, including *Keys to the Woody Plants of New Jersey* and *Trees and Shrubs in Eastern North America*, and teaching at Drew University.

Hal Tubbs was an affable man, very popular and at the center of what was a vibrant gardening circle in central New Jersey. He counted as friends Leonard and Helen Buck of

Allwood (now the Leonard J. Buck Garden), as well as Julia Newbold Cross of the Cross estate and his immediate neighbor and frequent walking companion, the landscape designer Martha Brookes Hutcheson of Bamboo Brook. Like his brother, he maintained a vast correspondence with leading plant collectors of his era, a correspondence continued and expanded by Blackburn.

By 1939 the Tubbses were already consciously developing Willowwood as an arboretum. Thirty years of collecting had resulted in the planting of a wide variety of woody plants, displayed with artistry in a series of gardens that visitors can still enjoy. Robert Tubbs died in 1942, but Hal Tubbs continued collecting and refining the garden, ably assisted by Ben Blackburn. Hal Tubbs eventually adopted Blackburn formally, and upon Tubbs's death in 1958 Blackburn became its steward. Tubbs had wanted the land and the garden to be open to the public, and in 1980 the Morris County Park Commission officially took ownership, with Blackburn remaining as director until his death in 1987.

Today the garden is unpretentious and welcoming, and a sense of delight in nature and plants pervades the place. The informal atmosphere remains, coupled with the meticulous documentation and extensive record-keeping that characterized the earlier iteration of the gardens. Over 2,000 different kinds of plants are maintained in the collections.

In front of the house, a cottage garden (originally the kitchen garden) features neat, rectangular, stone-edged beds, Ilex 'Sky Pencil' for structure, and a riot of bulbs and perennials overflowing the beds. It is an excellent example of Hal Tubbs's garden philosophy: a certain amount of structure is important to comfort the eye but plants should look at ease in their home. The central axis of the cottage garden continues through the house to the back where Hal Tubbs designed a more formal garden with intricate beds on either side of a grass panel, which extends down the axis and terminates at a statue of Pan. The grass panel tapers slightly to force the perspective. Originally a sunny, open garden with silvery plants like lamb's ears, inspired by the patterns in Persian carpets, it has been reconsidered as a white garden with plants arranged in an interwoven tapestry, but the concept of a somewhat formal, classical vista, designed to be contemplated in the evening from the back porch, remains the same.

Very early in their tenure the Tubbs brothers, who had a water garden as children, developed the brook, damming it to create the cypress pool and building a watercourse and edging the banks with stone. One of the first trees they planted was a bald cypress (Taxodium distichum), and they followed it with other more exotic cypress, magnolia and bamboo. Today, the woods walk, with its peculiar cypress "knees" popping up through the thick woodland, looks entirely natural, and it is only by identifying the vast range of plants—the now ancient Asian maples, Korean dogwoods, snowbells, Katsuras, to name but a few—that visitors realize that these plants are definitely not native to central New Jersey.

Dr. Blackburn continued to add specimens to the collection and to create gardens, among them the Rosarie, created in the 1960s and 1970s, which features the Mediterranean plants he grew to love during trips he and Hal took through that region.

Willowwood hosts important collections of maple, hickory, dogwood, magnolia, cherries, and lilacs. Displayed through the grounds in the most naturalistic of settings, it is easy to forget that they have been painstakingly catalogued and form a real scientific collection. Some of the specimens are of startling age and girth, like the massive Georgia pecan (Carya illinoinensis) at the entrance of the driveway, or the dawn redwood (Metasequoia glyptostroboides) planted in 1950 from seed collected on the famous 1947 Chinese expedition where the species was rediscovered and reintroduced to cultivation. Willowwood remains the garden legacy of the Tubbs brothers and Benjamin Blackburn. The particular zeitgeist of the garden seems to have been transmitted to following generations and it remains both an idiosyncratic and aesthetically satisfying meditation on the delights of the natural world.

Above: The rosarie, featuring plants from the Mediterranean region, was created by Dr. Blackburn in the 1960s and 1970s.

Opposite: Fastigiate hollies (Ilex crenata 'Sky Pencil') line the path of the present-day cottage garden, formerly the Tubbs's kitchen garden.

Overleaf: On the right, Lilac 'Lamartine' is part of Willowwood's extensive lilac collection, as is the tree silhouetted in the center, the Chinese tree lilac (Syringa pekinensis), which was planted in 1952. The white-flowered crabapple on the left (Malus 'Red Jade') dates from 1953.

Right and opposite: "Knees" from bald cypress (Taxodium distichum) probably planted in the early 1920s.

THE HAY, HONEY FARM

FAR HILLS

The comma in The Hay, Honey Farm is not a typo—it's a pun. Soon after the owner and his wife, after a long search, acquired this former cattle farm on the north branch of the Raritan River, they hired young horticulturists Michael and Hilary Clayton. As Hilary explains, "Early on it was agreed that there would be crops of hay and honey, and with a married couple working to create a garden for another married couple, there was plenty of 'Hey, honey' too." That was in 1989. More than two decades later the farm still produces hay and honey, but it is better known for the ten acres of gardens that surround the houses and barns on the valley floor and spread up the surrounding hillside.

From the beginning the owners knew that they wanted gardens, perhaps a woodland rhododendron walk, and a walled garden, but there was never a master plan. With the exception of the perennial border and the extensive vegetable and cutting gardens near the barns, the underlying approach has been to opt for diversity rather than large masses of the same plant. Over the years the number and kinds of plants have steadily increased and garden areas have proliferated, the owners guiding the direction of the expansion, the Claytons creating the gardens. Hilary Clayton focuses on the vegetables and perennials, Michael on the trees, and they share the shrubs. The plantings are laid out naturalistically, without allées or hedging or formal axes but, as Michael Clayton explains, "we tend to find a plant we like, and try and find the right spot for it." Early on, while the main house was being rebuilt, the Claytons were able to do significant prep work, especially improving the drainage and installing irrigation, which has stood them in good stead as the gardens have grown in scale.

A bulb, groundcover, and dwarf conifer garden, originally designed by Signe Nielsen, is nestled right up to the house for convenient viewing in early spring. A pink flowering Kentucky coffee tree (Cladastrus lutea) provides the vertical element. When the brilliant show of spring ephemerals dies back, the textures of the groundcovers and the dwarf conifers provide a subtler interest, and the main focus from the house moves farther away, to a wide, curved stone wall built into the hillside. The wall, designed and constructed by Bruce Crawford, now the director of the Rutgers Gardens, serves as the

Above: The ancient cherry tree frames a meadow of naturalized narcissus.

Opposite: Spring bulbs and ephemerals will give way to groundcovers in the garden by the house.

Overleaf: The curved perennial bed is still vibrant in the early fall. Large stands of perennials, like Joe-Pye weed, ensure that the bed is effective from a distance.

157

backdrop for an unusually deep and wide perennial border. It starts flowering in late spring but really comes into its own in the summer and fall months. Groupings of large-scale perennials like Joe-Pye weed and yellow scabious (Cephalaria gigantea) ensure that its impact is felt from far away.

A flowering shrub walk edges one of the rolling hayfields. The walk features sun-lovers like weigela, heptacodium and viburnum and eight lilac beds. The owners love lilacs and moved a number of existing ones to new spots that better suited their cultural needs. They have also added different cultivars to the collection. According to Michael Clayton, one of the secrets of the lilacs' robust health and flowering is severe pruning and annual deadheading. The deadheading is also one of the secrets of Hay, Honey's truly remarkable rhododendron display. Rhodondendrons have been an ongoing passion for the owners. More than two hundred cultivars have been artfully planted and appear to have naturally sprung up along a woodland path beside a small stream, and the collection is still growing. Another reason for the exceptional health of the rhododen-drons is the twenty years' worth of leaf mulch that increases the organic matter in the soil, a layer of groundcovers to keep the soil cool, and discreet irrigation that provides the steady moisture that these acid lovers prefer. By design, the rhododendron garden never peaks, but shows some color from April through June, and texture year-round.

The carefully managed wooded areas, painstakingly cleared of scourges like bitter-sweet, barberry and multiflora rose, are now filled with wild flowers and ground-covers, which cohabitate with the rhododendrons and the many uncommon species and cultivars that make up Hay, Honey's wide-ranging plant collection. Treasures like the woodland peony (Peony obovata), choice hostas, bloodroot (Sanguinaria canaden-sis), Allegheny spurge (Pachysandra procumbens) and the rare and beautiful Japanese wood poppy (Glaucidium palmatum) abound, each carefully sited with their cultural requirements as well as aesthetics in mind.

The owners have a close relationship with the Morris Arboretum in Pennsylvania and as a result Hay, Honey trials trees for them, often Asian versions of North American natives. Close attention to the woodland reveals all sorts of attractive but rarely seen cultivars, like the tall Stewartia (Stewartia monadelpha), a Chinese relation of our native

Above: Leucojum, narcissus and the double tulip 'Mt Tacoma'.

Opposite: Peeling bark of Heptacodium amid spring bloom.

Left: Rhododendron 'Olga Mezzit' in the woodland garden.

Opposite: Gourds hanging from the arched pergola in the extensive vegetable garden.

Stewartia, or Henry's Maple (Acer Henryi), a tri-lobed, small Asian maple, comfortably growing as if they had always inhabited the woodland in central New Jersey. Hay, Honey has an exceptional conifer collection with special emphasis on pines and firs, and the garden is still expanding. At Hay, Honey, there are always more fabulous plants to collect, and more perfect spots to put them in.

BIRD HAVEN FARM

TEWKSBURY TOWNSHIP

The first weekend Janet Mavec spent at Bird Haven Farm as a guest of Wayne Nordberg she asked him about his vegetable garden, and he replied that it was out of control. "Well," she volunteered, "I'll help you sometime." Little did he know where that "helping" would lead. The couple married in 1997, and Mavec joined in the stewardship of the property, which included a 100-acre farm of hayfields and orchards, three houses, a spring house, and two handsome barns. Even with a background in design, she couldn't figure out how to knit the myriad elements together. "It was like seven people at a table who didn't speak to one another," she remembers.

Mavec lived there for five years before she happened upon a book about Spanish architect and landscape designer Fernando Caruncho, whose poetic landscapes were much better known in Europe than in North America. This was the sensibility she had been looking for. With the help of architect Manuel Fernandez-Casteleiro, who had converted a rotting Sears kit house on the property to a modernist gem, she engaged Caruncho.

Above: A Japanese-inspired pavilion sits on the edge of a quiet pond.

Opposite: The monastery garden beside the barn.

To Caruncho, the messy set of buildings brought to mind a medieval village, and from this idea he developed the master plan for twenty-five acres. At its heart is the town center, a gravel courtyard with a circular pool set in front of the eighteenth-century stone cottage. The gardens, houses, and barns radiate out from it, with the great sweep of the sloping field providing protection for the little village.

Nordberg and Mavec didn't implement all of the master plan, deeming some of it too grand and too bold. They wanted a farm, not an estate, and, in fact, the hayfields and orchard continue to be productive. But they liked the central conceit that knit the disparate pieces together. Within this framework, Mavec and Nordberg were able to plan a varied series of gardens. There is an exuberant potager, designed by Lisa Stamm, with vegetables as well as perennial beds. Lisa's husband, Dale Booher, designed the encircling walls and chic deer fence. In the barnyard, where the old dog pen used to be, they created the "monastery" garden of clipped box and santolina, inspired in part by

Right and opposite: Fernando Caruncho's design links the disparate elements of the farm by focusing on a reflecting pool in the courtyard as the center of the composition. Seen from the top of the hill, the house and barn complex have echoes of a medieval village.

Overleaf: Perennials are interspersed with vegetables in the exuberant potager. The planting is reimagined each year.

the cloisters at Santa Maria Novella in Florence. A woodland walk passes by a sizable bed of hellebores. Nearby, a Japanese-inspired pavilion (designed by Manuel Fernandez-Casteleiro) provides a quiet place to sit overlooking the pond.

A diagonal path leads to the top of the field where Caruncho had wanted to build a giant viewing mound. The rustic pavilion there now is much more modest and in scale with the buildings below. But the view down the field to the huddle of barns and houses bound by a stone wall does indeed evoke an ancient village, and the buildings are finally having a conversation.

Above: In most years, the apple orchard is highly productive.

Opposite: Rock outcroppings tie in with beautifully crafted stone walls.

JARDIN DE BUIS

POTTERSVILLE

Over a period of twenty years, architect Andrea Filippone has transformed an abandoned dairy farm in the Hunterdon hills into a magical complex of indoor and outdoor living spaces, reminiscent of a French provincial farmstead, but clearly rooted in the local countryside. Although trained in contemporary modernist practice, her imagination is fired by the romance and patina of old objects and a deep feeling for New Jersey's vanishing landscape.

The garden is informed by Filippone's affinity for French garden architecture, by her extensive collection of architectural salvage, and by the large herds of deer that roam the surrounding hills. A decision early on that fencing the large property wasn't feasible meant that the plantings would be limited to deer-proof species. Filippone has turned this to advantage: disparate garden rooms are linked by a shared and restrained plant palette, carefully chosen to soften the sharp edges of her classically laid out gardens. Large groupings of nepeta sway atop die-straight stone walls, frothing lady's mantle softens corners and blurs edges, but the most important plant in the design scheme is boxwood.

Filippone is passionate about boxwood. In fact she named her garden after it—Jardin de Buis means Garden of Boxwood. It forms the backbone of most of her designs, ensuring that they work as well in the winter as in other seasons, and she has a sizable boxwood nursery on the thirty-five-acre property. She never clips it. Instead she uses varieties that grow to the shape she wants in each design, delighting in the differences in contour of leaf, color, and habit of the twenty-five varieties she has planted.

Above: This garden was designed as the view from the kitchen. The boxwood encloses Brunnera 'Jack Frost.' The urn holds a fucraea.

Opposite: Architectural salvage lends character to each garden area. Here, bluestone pavers, worn from years of use, are repurposed as the surround for the pool.

Her large collection of salvage artifacts is displayed throughout the ten acres of gardened land. Old iron gates, finials, bits of decorative ironwork, stone planters, and reused stone pavers are seamlessly integrated into the designs. The property is extensively terraced, and most of the stone used in the retaining walls comes from the property.

From the very beginning Filippone wanted a potager. Two six-foot fences set ten feet apart, one privet and one a wooden trellis pattern inspired by Versailles, were installed to deter the deer. Filippone often uses an object from the past as a jumping-off point

Above and right: The trellis
walls of the potager were
inspired by trellis at Versailles.
The cobblestone paving was
found in Philadelphia. The
design of the beds changes
every year.

for her designs. The departure point here was a load of eighteenth-century cobbles she found in Philadelphia, which she used as paving. The square beds, edged in boxwood, are redesigned and replanted every year.

The greenhouse garden lies on axis from the center point of the potager: two wings of greenhouse joined by an orangerie enclose a simple gravel garden with a swimming pool as the main water feature. The greenhouses, originally from the biology labs at Rutgers University, were reassembled over two years and serve to overwinter the growing collection of agaves (chosen partially because the deer hate them), among other choice specimens that fill the pots throughout the gardens in the summer.

In addition to her love of boxwood and historical objects, Filippone has become deeply committed to environmental design and soil health. It started with concern for the health of her beloved boxwood and frustration at the limitations of her clay soil, but she has come to realize that improving the soil first simplifies the problem-solving in the garden long-term. For a visitor, however, there are no perceivable problems in her garden. It is surprisingly of the moment—shaped by a twenty-first century voice and warmed by the patina of age.

Above: The orangerie links the two greenhouse wings.

Opposite: The greenhouses were discarded by Rutgers University and reassembled here.

Overleaf: The boxwood (Buxus sinica var. 'Justin Brouwers') in the white garden is never clipped. The pillowy shape is its natural habit.

Above, left: Agave (used extensively because the deer do not eat them) in a cast-iron urn from France.

Above, right: Architectural elements are placed throughout the grounds.

Opposite: Much of the stone in the extensive network of walls was found on the property. The nepeta is 'Walker's Low.'

GARDEN IN
TEWKSBURY TOWNSHIP

Set on top of a hill, with views that stretch for miles, these gardens have the old-fashioned charm of a family place that has been lovingly tended for generations. For the current owner, who grew up here, this is home in a way that no other place can be. Memories of her mother are always present in gardens filled with peony, iris, and lilac. Changes have been made over the years but only to enhance the property, never to stray too far from its original character.

The garden areas are clustered around the house, giving a sense of welcome enclosure after the long drive through open hayfields. A two-story double porch at the south side of the house overlooks a small private garden whose outer walls are made up of two-hundred-year-old English boxwood that block the wind. In front of the boxwood are deep beds planted with a range of perennials with long-lasting color—Russian sage, asters, echinacea, Japanese anemones, sedum, pansies, iris, and peonies. A similar planting scheme is used on the long perennial beds at the back of the house, although there the swaths of spring-blooming peonies and Siberian iris predominate.

The south-facing vegetable garden was recently redesigned after much thought and the sharing of ideas by the owners and garden designer Shelby Doggett Mellick, who then translated it all into a pleasing and cohesive landscape. The garden fits in beautifully, with its Victorian fence, orderly raised bluestone beds, peastone paths, and an antique iron fountain surrounded by zinnias and herbs. It may look as though the garden was meant to be primarily ornamental, but it was specifically designed for serious organic production—especially for growing large quantities of Jersey tomatoes and basil for more than 150 quarts of juice, tomato sauce, and pesto. In addition, beets, lima beans, spinach, leeks, garlic, peas, shallots, French beans, fennel, specialty lettuces and every herb imaginable are grown for family and friends. Shaded by vines of hyacinth bean and morning glory, the nineteenth-century iron sink, found in an architectural salvage shop, is flanked by potting tables handcrafted by one of the owners in his workshop on the property.

Above: The potting bench and sink in the corner of the vegetable garden.

Opposite: Perennial beds line the fence that separates the back lawn from the orchard.

Overleaf: The extensive vegetable garden abuts the hayfields.

Left: Rows of tomatoes edged with marigolds ripen in the vegetable garden.

Opposite: The garden affords expansive views of the surrounding farmland.

The extensive hayfields and apple orchards surrounding the house offer a spectacular long view. Planted with cool-season grasses, the hayfields are also an important habitat for grassland birds. Mowing is only permitted after mid-July to give the nesting birds a chance to raise their young. The fields are filled with Bobolinks, Meadowlark, Savannah Sparrows, and Grasshopper Sparrows, all of which are on the threatened or endangered list for New Jersey. Bluebirds flash across the fields and gardens; kestrels successfully fledge new chicks year after year from the specially built Audubon box. It would seem that not only the owners call this tranquil place home.

FAIRFIELDS

OLDWICK

When Basil and Rilda Hone first walked up the hill in the mid-1980s to look at a piece of land on this hillside, they were greeted by a small group of cows in a very muddy field. Beyond the field, though, was a spectacular, panoramic view north across hayfields to the hills in the distance. The open sky, with its play of light, reminded them of the skies in their native southern Africa and seemed the perfect backdrop to the house and garden that they wanted to build for their retirement.

The brief that the Hones gave their son, Keith, who had just graduated from architecture school, was to design a house that looked like a barn and would blend in with the two large nineteenth-century barns on either side of the property. The resulting house and accompanying silo look as though they are reconditioned farm buildings and completely suit the setting. The only problem was that, as Rilda Hone says, "barns don't have gardens" and she knew she wanted a garden. Having grown up in South Africa in the formal, English-style gardens of her mother and grandmother, she had always been drawn to gardens where structure and symmetry were important, but clearly this site required something very different.

Above: The narrow lap pool overlooks the valley below.

Opposite: Large groupings of Miscanthus mark the curve in the driveway on the way to the house.

Hone decided to use ornamental grasses almost exclusively: they move in the wind and pick up the light that streaks across the property, creating an exciting yet naturalistic foreground to the distant view beyond. She started out with just a few varieties, but the palette has expanded over the years until now there are over twenty different varieties of grasses, such as Miscanthus, Pennisetum, and Calamagrostis. The grasses peak in September when the seed heads form, but Hone's favorite time in the garden is July, when the grasses are just forming up and before they have gotten too top heavy.

Meadow plants like Joe-Pye weed and several forms of butterfly bush are used to accent many of the beds, and purple-flowering verbena bonariensis has seeded itself everywhere, providing late-season color and attracting a large variety of butterflies (including the endangered Monarchs). The grasses and meadow plants are all deer resistant, which is an important consideration in this part of New Jersey where marauding deer are a constant problem. The lap pool was designed to evoke a South African cattle dip, with grasses planted right up to the edge.

The huge view is inevitably the dominant organizing force, and the well-established grasses are of a scale that complements it. Very little has been added over the years. The only tree that the Hones have planted is a copper beech, now over thirty feet tall, a gift from Basil Hone on his wife's birthday soon after they moved in, which he says is his only contribution to her creation. Two pieces of sculpture have been thoughtfully placed in the landscape: a hollow ceramic ball and a bird by Italian sculptor Stella Magni, which was once in the South African garden of Rilda Hone's mother. Yet the most essential element of this garden is surely the sky itself—the clouds that gather and shift and the stars at night that seem almost close enough to touch—an ever-present reminder of the skies of southern Africa.

Above: Verbena bonariensis has seeded itself throughout the property.

Opposite: The mature copper beech provides a contrast of color and texture.

Overleaf: The massive plantings of mixed grasses balance the view.

FEDERAL TWIST

KINGWOOD TOWNSHIP

James Golden had already been gardening for many years before he and his husband, Phillip Saperia, decided to make this house on Federal Twist Road their new home. The one-story 1960s split ranch with its large picture windows, designed by William Hunt, a notable New Jersey architect, was the perfect setting for their collection of decorative arts by local artists and artisans. But the three and one-half acre landscape was a real challenge—a tangled mess of junipers and weed trees and heavy, wet clay soil. Golden, who had recently discovered the work of the Dutch garden designer Piet Oudolf and the writer Noel Kingsbury and, through Kingsbury, the German habitat-influenced perennials movement, wanted to try his hand at creating a naturalistic garden. He started to experiment with different plants to see what would thrive on this difficult site. Now, eight years since he started clearing the land and thousands of seedlings later, the result is a layered, complex prairie-style planting that changes dramatically with the seasons.

A narrow, south-facing terrace running the length of the house overlooks the open, expansive, sloping garden, where something is always happening. "It starts as an absolutely bare field in late March, quickly gains green texture and form as spring advances, morphs into a dreamscape of flowering spires and mounds in late summer, then takes on glorious reds, browns, russets, and oranges as the late grasses flower in late fall," Golden explains. "Most plants are highly structural and remain standing through winter to catch early morning hoar frosts and snow, making a long-lasting winter landscape." A wide gravel path encircles the garden, and the intersecting, narrow mowed paths invite further wandering. There are stopping points along the way—in one opening, which serves as a tiny secret garden, a pair of Wave Hill chairs hide in tall Silphium and Inula; in another, a rectangular pool with dyed black water reflects the sky.

The seriousness with which Golden has studied the art of prairie planting is balanced by the evident fondness that he has for each and every one of the varieties that he has planted. He uses a restrained palette of tough, competitive plants, and he is particularly pleased when he sees them self-seed, establishing new colonies in odd places in the garden. One of his favorite self-seeders is the non-native Inula racemosa: its golden blooms

Above and opposite: A sculpture by Marc Rosenquist in the midst of extravagant midsummer blooms and again in the fall.

Above: Adirondack chairs on the back terrace looking southeast over the garden on the hillside below.

Opposite: Wave Hill chairs hidden among Silphium perfoliatum and Vernonia.

Overleaf: Friends gave Golden seed balls one year, and these rudbeckia have been re-seeding and blooming ever since.

wave high in the late summer and its strong structure keeps it upright throughout the winter. The Inula was also a favorite plant of another garden mentor of Golden's, Wolfgang Oehme, the landscape architect who was known for his sweeps of distinctive perennial plants.

Golden's artificial prairie is an evolving landscape, and disturbance is a natural part of the evolution. In 2012 high winds during Hurricane Sandy knocked down seventeen mature white pines that marked the edge of the garden. Since they were on neighboring conserved land, Golden had to leave them where they had fallen, but he is watching carefully to see what will grow in the newly sunny part of the garden. This is far from a passive, low-maintenance process. As he has done throughout his property, he will constantly edit to maintain an ideal balance of color and texture and form, and the reward will be a sensitive composition that brings to mind Henry David Thoreau's quote: "In Wildness is the preservation of the world."

FROG POND

PRINCETON

In thirty-two years of considered gardening, Katie Heins developed a sure sense of what was right for her garden and acquired a deep lode of horticultural expertise. The exceptional garden she built in Princeton is a model of serenity and quiet beauty, where there are no jarring moments and each plant blends sensitively into the composition. It is entirely appropriate for the woodland setting, for the handsome 1950s brick house, and for the hands-on gardener who has risen to become the national president of the Garden Club of America.

She will tell you that it has taken more than thirty years to achieve this level of excellence. When she moved to the property, there were some azaleas in front of the house and a grassy area and pond in the back, but other-wise the second-growth woods, clogged with honeysuckle, grew right up to the edge of the small lawn. As a novice gardener, she struggled with the clay soil, and her win-lose ratio in new planting was woefully unbalanced. A three-year course at the demanding Barnes Foundation Arboretum School taught her the value of improving the soil on the one hand, and the folly of trying to impose a plant on the landscape on the other. These lessons learned, her mantra became "right plant, right place," and her garden took off. At the same time her work with the Garden Club of America afforded her the opportunity to visit many of the best gardens in the country, honing her already acute eye.

Heins was drawn to the subtle and often fleeting pleasures of the woodland, and much of the focus in this garden is on a gently curving gravel path that winds through a wood. It all looks very natural but on closer inspection it is packed with precious specimens. The garden awakens in very early spring with the odd early azalea and several magnifi-cent witch hazels and builds to a crescendo in mid-spring when the woods fairly glow with the brilliant green young foliage of the trees and ferns, and a carpet of tiny bulbs spreads across the forest floor. If one looks for rareties, there are many, like the fleeting woodland Peony obovata or the Dodecatheon, a charming, underused bulb. But it is the overall effect of freshness and light that is so beguiling.

Most of the plants have a brief show in the spring and are quiet the rest of the year, so the texture of the leaf, and the structure and shape of the plant become very important. A close reading reveals the care with which a substantial hosta leaf is placed beside a

Above: A weeping cherry reflected in the pond.

Opposite: A colorful mixed bulb display in the perennial beds by the house contrasts with the quieter tones of the woodland beyond.

lacy fern. This attention to texture is even more important in the overstory: a stand of Cryptomeria create an important island in the lawn, and the unusual grain of their foliage draws the eye and forms an agreeable contrast to the canopy of deciduous native forest. Elsewhere, the long, peeling strips of the shagbark hickory become the focal point of a composition.

Heins developed a series of perennial plantings on the terraces surrounding the house. These borders are more formal and assertive than the woodland, and there is an interesting change of mood between the two, with the small lawn acting as transitional space. Scattered around the property, especially close to the house, are a series of troughs and subtly planted pots. These aren't used to add dashes of color to the garden but rather to add a quality of refinement to the composition. Each is an exquisite object and the plants in them are carefully chosen to complement the pot's design.

In proportion to the garden, the pond seems large and perfectly balances the scale of the woodland. As the forest grows progressively denser and darker in the run up to high summer, the pond remains restfully wide open and the carefully chosen specimens that surround it are reflected in the summer sky.

Above: The woodland peony (Paeonia obovata) blooms near a stand of Virginia bluebells (Mertensia virginica).

Opposite: Japanese primrose at the foot of a stand of Cryptomeria chosen for textural contrast with the native trees that surround it.

Overleaf: The Japanese-influenced gravel path winding through a stand of shooting star (Dodecatheon meadia).

BOXWOOD COTTAGE

PRINCETON

When Elizabeth Wislar bought this property fifteen years ago, there was nothing here: the neglected grounds around the run-down cottage were flat and featureless with only three plants. But for Wislar it was a blank slate and just what she was looking for. The L-shaped lot wrapped around the house in a friendly way, and she saw its potential. It took a year to get the permits for a deer fence, and during that time she meticulously planned a garden, envisioning three distinct rooms—a formal north garden, a rectangular croquet lawn that would encompass the cocktail and dining areas, and a working garden and compost room.

Inspired by her grandparents' Southern garden, she renamed her place Boxwood Cottage. Then she set about finding a boxwood guru. She joined the Boxwood Society of America, and went to Washington, D.C. for their annual meeting, making friends among the mostly Southern growers who attended. By the time she was ready to install the formal north garden, she knew her boxwood and chose the variety Justin Brouwers for the main hedges.

Wislar is one of those remarkable people who can clearly see the mature garden as she is designing it. Today the garden has grown up and it is just how she imagined it would be fifteen years ago. She installed it herself and all the plants, including the boxwood, went into the ground as tiny starts. The tall European hornbeam hedge that divides the formal north garden from the croquet lawn looked like what Wislar describes as a "line of Q-tips" when she planted them; she pleached them by tying the branches to bamboo poles, forcing them to grow in the traditional squared-off shape. Knowing that she would maintain the garden herself, and understanding that herbaceous plants can be very exacting, Wislar opted for a quiet green garden of shrubs and trees. In the main garden, the site of many summer croquet games, the shrubs are all white-flowering, "clean and restful," in her words, and light up the evening.

There are two major exceptions to the quiet palette. In spring, the box-bordered beds in the north garden are filled with Coral Charm peonies, accented by grace notes of purple allium. Each year, Wislar watches the coral petals emerge from the chartreuse foliage, waiting until the golden stamens add their exclamation points to the huge

Above: This wisteria by the kitchen door was one of only three existing plants when Wislar bought the cottage.

Opposite: Wislar pleached the European hornbeam hedge herself and planted all the boxwood.

flower heads; once she can pinpoint perfection, she invites friends for an impromptu peony party to share the magnificent sight. The other exception also inspires a gathering. When she bought the cottage, one of the three existing plants was the wisteria that grew by the kitchen door. Having always wanted to have wisteria, she waited with mounting anticipation for it to bloom. Spring came and went without a single blossom. Research revealed that the plant needed to be severely root-pruned. The pruning coupled with the loss of a tree shading the doorway provided the perfect environment and, right on cue, the next spring, and each one thereafter, the kitchen door has been draped with hundreds of fragrant wisteria blossoms. Wislar's friends are invited to celebrate with "dinner on the driveway."

Left and opposite: The Coral Charm peonies with purple allium make an extravagant show in late spring. The formal edging is Justin Brouwers boxwood.

LINDEN HILL

RUMSON

For a very colorful summer garden, annuals are a must. At Linden Hill, the summer display of pyrotechnic intensity is a twenty-seven-year tradition. Never less than 45,000 and in some years as many as 75,000 annuals ignite the grounds in July and August. Set within the framework of an extensive collection of trees, the flowers create a cheerful kaleidoscope that pulls the eye right through the property. Remarkably, the summer display is almost entirely grown in greenhouses on the property. It is a traditional—some might think old-fashioned—approach to gardening that suited the owners of the garden, Gene Mercy and his late wife, Sue, and their longtime gardener, Clive Deeble.

The Mercys lived in New York and spent summers in Rumson. Sue Mercy wanted color and warmth in her summer garden, and Clive was happy to oblige. In the spring, two thousand tulips, in addition to thousands of daffodils, complement a vivid azalea moment. A fine collection of magnolias edges the drive, and a rock garden provides horticultural focus in late spring. But the personality of the garden is defined by the exuberant summer show, with beds bursting with color, and zinnias, begonias, salvias, nicotianas, and snapdragons, to name but a few, jostling each other and competing for attention.

Above and opposite: At least 45,000 annuals go into the garden each year. Most of them are started in greenhouses on the property.

The sheer wattage of all those shapes and colors would be overwhelming if it were not for the impeccable grooming of the garden backdrop, which is highly controlled. Grass is perfectly cropped at all times, the beds are edged and cultivated every week, shrubs are well pruned. This discipline contrasts with the relative chaos of the annuals' colors and shapes and results in a garden of exceptional energy.

The collaboration between the Mercys and Clive Deeble started in 1985 when Clive, an Englishman who had been trained at two horticultural colleges in England, came to work for them. They had recently bought the property and had commissioned Steven Krog, a local landscape architect, to design a master plan and install the now fully mature perimeter planting. Clive then took over, gradually adding beds and plants. He started with the view from the Mercys' bedroom, creating an island bed with two ponds, and worked outward, planting small specimen trees and giving them room to grow. When Sue Mercy requested a dry stone wall for a proposed bed, Clive brought

his father, Edgar Charles Deeble, over from England one summer. He built a two-level 96-foot-long wall that retains one of the main flower beds.

Between the Mercys' vision and Clive's ability, the tree collection grew enormously. In addition to the magnolia collection, which includes Elizabeth, Ballerina, and Galaxy, there are two magnificent Parrotia persica, planted long before these were well-known garden trees, a Japanese snowbell, a Stewartia, and an Umbrella pine as well as Contorted pine and Thujopsis, not to mention the usual suspects like dogwood, beech, maple, birch, and any number of conifers. Apples and pears neatly arranged in an orchard provide ample fruit for friends and neighbors.

Wherever the Mercys went they searched for inspiration for the garden, and they used to joke that Clive could grow anything. Once they came back from a weekend in Long Island with a tiny slip of Cryptomeria and handed it over. Clive thought to himself that he might have overstated his abilities, but that tiny slip is now a huge and handsome tree, its idiosyncratic needle pattern adding important texture to the green framework of the garden. The Mercy garden is a testament to collaboration, enthusiasm, even love for the garden, and an increasingly rare ingredient, a traditionally trained expert gardener, who can grow 75,000 annuals or a Cryptomeria from a tiny slip.

Right and opposite: Closely
cropped lawn and a backdrop
of grasses and trees gives
structure to the profusion of
color and shape of the plants.

POODLE POINT

RUMSON

Ann Unterberg likes straight lines and squares, and each of the garden rooms at the property she shares with her family reflects this bias. She also likes soft edges, romantic colors and old-fashioned flowers, and the garden reflects this as well. It is the combination of these strongly held preferences that gives this garden its decided personality.

Twenty years ago the Unterbergs bought a Victorian house on a long narrow lot on the banks of the Navesink River. Ann Unterberg's preferences were clear—she wanted something at once country and architectural—so they removed the grand entrance gates and planted an orchard in rows. Twenty years later there are almost fifty meticulously shaped apple trees and narrow beds of dusty blue Walker's Low nepeta trace rectangles underneath the trees, extending seasonal interest and also making the pattern of rows and squares slightly more complex. This was the first room of their outdoor "house."

Next, they turned their attention to the gatehouse set deep into the property, which, in the Unterbergs' view, needed to be linked with the house. They built a pergola, creating a rectangular garden room between the gatehouse and the main house where the idea was a formal garden with fluffy, relaxed plants. And, because Ann Unterberg loves roses, roses would be the main focus. At first, they were mostly hybrid teas and David Austin selections but, over the years, practicality has dictated adding a number of newer, less finicky varieties. The rows of roses are interspersed with hydrangeas, and a mixed shrub, grass and perennial border edges the garden on one side, filled with "plants that work"—hydrangeas, lythrums, geraniums, dahlias. The effect is, as intended, one of formal orthogonal shape, and billowy planting.

When the Unterbergs acquired the property next door, they extended the orchard across both lots, but retained a large lawn on the new property marked by two huge box balls. This garden room has become the play space, an elegant enclosure for everything from soccer to croquet. They built a guest house on this second property; the front porch, edged with a blue hydrangea hedge, has a long view across the Navesink River. To solve

Above: A perennial planting by the pool area.

Opposite: Unterberg's preference for geometry is evident in the bird's eye view of the rose garden.

Opposite, above: Huge box balls add formality to the lawn, which also serves as a play space.

Opposite, below: The pergola and rose garden, seen from near the entrance to the "plaid garden." The roses are deadheaded weekly, ensuring continuous bloom from May to October.

Overleaf: A view over hydrangea 'Nikko Blue' to the Navesink River.

Above: In the "plaid garden" boxwood and red barberry form interlocking squares; the pattern is emphasized by the brick and bluestone paving.

the problem of linking the two main houses together, the Unterbergs turned to landscape architect Claudia Levy, who designed the space they call the "plaid garden," a wonderfully complex garden of interlocking squares with large serviceberries anchoring the center of each square. Two kinds of boxwood at two different heights and red barberry created the formal structure, while gooseneck loosestrife, St. John's wort, daylilies and nepeta add a little airiness to the mix. The boxwood is drop-crotch-pruned by hand (in fact, all the pruning on the property is done by hand), so the shape is clear, but not razor sharp. The paving, bluestone with strips of red brick laid end to end, completes the pattern. It is a tour de force, and the ultimate expression of the approach that underlies all these garden rooms: each garden is like an architectural drawing executed with a charcoal pencil—entirely rational, but softened by the plant palette of seaside favorites.

LINWOOD ARBORETUM

LINWOOD

When the noted garden writer Allen Lacy first met J. C. Raulston, the preeminent plantsman of his generation, he said to him, "I'm not particularly interested in woody plants." Raulston replied, "You will be." Lacy, who has worn many hats—including those of professor of philosophy and professor of horticulture (at the same time) at Richard Stockton College, where in 1970 he was a founding faculty member—did become passionate about woody plants. Ultimately he came to share Raulston's evangelical zeal for expanding the plant palettes of ordinary Americans, thus improving countless front yards and civic spaces.

Raulston founded the ten-acre arboretum that now bears his name at North Carolina State University, which has become one of the most influential in the country. Following in his footsteps, in 2008 Lacy and a few like-minded colleagues created a tiny arboretum in Linwood. At under an acre it's probably the smallest in the United States, but the Friends of Linwood Arboretum hopes to influence a whole generation of townspeople and in so doing increase the diversity of landscape plant material in southern New Jersey and beyond.

Above: A white buddleia 'White Ball' is placed near the trunk of the Japanese apricot (Prunus mume).

Opposite: The chartreuse leaves of the sumac (Rhus typhina 'Tiger Eye') contrast with the pawpaw (Asimina trilobite), bayberry (Myrica pennsylvanica), a white-flowered hibiscus (Hybiscus moscheutos 'Kopper King'),and the seed pods of butterfly weed (Asclepias tuberosa).

In 2007, the Linwood city council was debating, not for the first time, what to do with a tiny scrap of land that used to hold an electrical substation, just down the street from the Lacy home. Lacy suggested an arboretum, after pointing out that it was much too small for a soccer field. Recognizing that the land was ideally situated for his mission of educating the public—it was a triangular lot across the street from a middle school and it abutted a bike path and a busy street, making it visible and accessible to the widest possible range of citizens—he was determined to transform the miserable bit of grass into a pleasing and instructional collection of plants. The arboretum's mission would be to include "only unique plants of exceptional interest," thus banning the ubiquitous Bradford pear and forsythia from the grounds. Fortunately, the city council agreed.

Bolstered by grants from the Atlantic County Open Spaces program and the city council. Lacy and his wife, Hella, his partner in life and horticulture, spent a most enjoyable

spring choosing specimens and building the collection. They were fortunate to have able colleagues: Doortje Fenwick, a local architect, drew up the plans for a stroll garden that would be a showcase for remarkable plants, and George Butrus, manager of a nearby plant nursery and the Linwood Shade Tree Commissioner, coordinated the planting.

Today, the arboretum, with its collection of over three hundred plants and many summer tropicals, is gratifyingly lush. Because most East Coast gardens focus on spring-blooming plants, Linwood emphasizes plants that show their colors in the other seasons and there is something blooming twelve months a year. The collection has a definite bias towards natives, but also frequently pairs them with East Asian species of the same genera. There is an emphasis on finding multiple forms of the same plant; for example, nine varieties of witch hazel light up the garden from Thanksgiving to early April, and thirteen different magnolias bloom from March until frost (one variety, for its prolonged season of sporadic bloom, is even called March till Frost). In a nod to the ecosystem of the nearby Pine Barrens, the arboretum features a raised bog garden focusing on native New Jersey carnivorous plants, mostly pitcher plants, many of which are endangered.

J. C. Raulston finished every letter with the motto "Plan and plant for a better America." The dedicated crew that created and now sustains the Linwood Arboretum takes pride in the fact that it is following his credo.

Opposite: The goal of the garden is to introduce new plants to local gardeners.

Above: Pitcher plant (Sarracenia flava) in the bog garden with driftwood.

PAT AND
CLAY SUTTON GARDEN

GOSHEN

Cape May County is not all beach umbrellas and gingerbread houses. This small peninsula with Delaware Bay on one side and the Atlantic Ocean on the other is also one of the foremost places in North America to see migrating birds and butterflies. In the spring and fall, dozens of species of butterflies and hundreds of species of birds—in particular, shorebirds, songbirds, and raptors— have been spotted stopping along the way to eat a good meal before flying on. They are particularly attracted to the peninsula's diverse habitat of wetlands, woodlands, and fields, and also to the hundreds of wildlife gardens throughout the county.

Pat and Clay Sutton, expert naturalists and educators, have turned their small backyard into tightly planted beds filled with delectable delights for migrating wildlife and for resident and wintering species too. When Pat sets off from her back door to show a visitor her garden she grabs her camera and binoculars— just in case she spots a guest. It might be a Monarch butterfly or a Ruby-throated Hummingbird or a small box turtle, but whatever it is, it will find a safe haven in Pat's garden with its wealth of native plants.

Above and opposite: A small pond is surrounded by midsummer blooms of purple coneflower and white phlox.

When the Suttons moved here in 1977, it was a bare lot less than half an acre in size. They began with a vegetable garden in the backyard but then one day a friend gave them some beebalm, which is a magnet for butterflies; once the butterflies came, Pat gave up on vegetables and threw herself into planting a garden that would attract wildlife. Years later, when the backyard was dug up for a new septic field, combining Clay's aesthetic sense and Pat's knowledge of plants, they created a new garden that is truly pleasing to the eye and not just a collection of wildlife-friendly plants.

The Suttons have packed several different habitats into the small space: two wildlife ponds, where leopard frogs live even in a summer of drought; a meadow, planted with milkweed, purple coneflower, asters, and little bluestem; and a small woodlot, "the back 40," where they have cleared out multiflora rose and Japanese honeysuckle to allow native plants to take hold. Beyond their half-acre lie hundreds of acres of land protected as part of the Cape May National Wildlife Refuge.

The staples of the garden include spring-blooming coral honeysuckle, wild columbine and coral bells; summer-blooming phlox, beebalm, rudbeckia, purple coneflower,
milkweeds, boneset, liatris and perennial salvia; and fall-blooming ironweed, asters,
goldenrod, Joe-Pye weed, sunflowers, sedum, and chelone. There are scary plants as
well, namely poison ivy and pokeweed, which are cultivated for their high quality food
(fifty different birds eat their berries). The carefully cultivated wildness is contained by
a living fence that has overrun the original chain-link fence and now doubles as a deer
barrier and wildlife corridor.

Above: In midsummer purple
coneflower and beebalm
overflow the beds.

Opposite: Swallowtail butterfly
feasting on the Joe-Pye weed.

HEREFORD INLET LIGHTHOUSE

NORTH WILDWOOD

Standing at the top of the Hereford Inlet Lighthouse looking out over the Atlantic Ocean you can almost imagine being the keeper of the light a hundred years ago. You would be watching for ships to warn them of the shallow inlet waters and all around you would be sand and water. Those days are long gone, and now the lighthouse is hemmed in on three sides by the busy beach town of North Wildwood, but the time-out-of-time quality is palpable from the moment one enters the lighthouse garden through the white picket fence.

The architect Paul J. Peltz, who was the chief draftsman for the U.S. Lighthouse Board and went on to design the Library of Congress in Washington, D.C., designed the lighthouse in the Swiss Carpenter Gothic, or stick, style, which was popular at the time. Erected in 1874, the picturesque lighthouse saw steady service until 1964, when modernization came in the form of an automatic, rotating light placed on a tower nearby. No longer useful, the lighthouse was closed and shuttered until it was rescued in 1982 by the city of North Wildwood. Restoration began immediately, and in 1986 the automated light was moved back into the lighthouse, making it fully functional again. In the same year, Steve Murray, who was then city superintendent of parks, started a small flower garden on the street side of the newly reopened lighthouse as part of his general landscaping duties. Over the years, Murray, who retired from his municipal job and is now chairman of the Friends of the Lighthouse, has planted more and more: the small border has grown to fill the grounds of the lighthouse and the highly decorative gardens are an attraction in and of themselves.

Above: Hereford Inlet Lighthouse is still in service, but it is also a museum.

Opposite: The garden is protected from the harsh ocean winds by a screen of Japanese black pine with chaste-tree (Vitex agnus-castus) in front.

In order to turn the barren landscape around the lighthouse into gardens, Murray knew he would first have to solve the problem of sand, which is so much better for sunbathing than for planting. He brought in tons of topsoil to add as much as ten inches to some garden beds. His next challenge was the wind, which he solved first with fencing, then by planting a screen of Japanese black pine underplanted with a mix of native shrubs, such as bayberry, beach plum and viburnum. He also installed a watering system, since he knew the wind, salt and summer sun would quickly dry out any plants he put in the ground.

Right: Colorful annuals spill over the beds and planters.

Opposite: Twenty-foot-tall purple chaste-tree (Vitex agnus-castus) in the boxwood-lined herb garden.

Overleaf: The gazebo in the garden is surrounded by varieties of hydrangea that thrive at the seashore.

Murray decided that a Victorian cottage garden would best complement the architecture of the lighthouse. Every year, he lays out the planting beds, choosing different flowers depending on availability from a long list of appropriate varieties. At its peak in late June and July, the cheerful profusion of the garden, with hundreds of candy-colored annuals winding through the beds of perennials and shrubs, is the horticultural highlight of summer at the shore.